THE FALLING STARS

AIMEN IQBAL

AURAQ

Printed in the Islamic Republic of Pakistan.
Printed: April, 2020
Edition: 1st
ISBN: 978-969-7868-92-6
Price: Rs 1,200 PKR, $12 US

ISLAMABAD, PAKISTAN

raabta@auraqpublications.com.pk | +92-300-0571-530
www.auraqpublications.com.pk | @AuraqPublications
ISBN : 978-969-7868-92-6

The light travels when the stars fall.

From the skies to the lands

And to the pages.

THE FALLING STARS.

What are you made of? I am made of stars that are continuously falling out of my open wounds. Some I push to fall for I have wishes to come true. Some fall when their tethering ropes give up its strength, exhausted by the agonies swelling my chest. And some- some are fated to fall.

What are you made of?

I am made of falling stars

DEDICATION NOTE:

Beginnings or endings? This statement has long tantalized me. There are times I want to kiss the face of magic when I step on the very threshold and sometimes, I want to leave the journey with my heart full.

Beginnings or endings? I don't know, readers. Indulged in this uncertainty, I'll begin this journey with the same name with which I'll end it.

To *Al-Muhyee* (The Giver of Life) who gave life to all the words which have ever left me and which will ever leave. Who gave life to the faith and belief in me; faith in His miracles and belief on the powers He had endowed my fingers with. Who gave life to my pen. Who gave life to my strength when the air which came into my lungs was shattering my bones. Who gave life to this book. Who gave life to me.

To all the people who had ever stopped to traverse through my poems and fables. To all the people who were inspired by me. To all the travelers of the roads of Karachi who had stopped to pass a smile or a word of blessing to me. To all the roads of Karachi themselves, especially the Saddar roads I ambled during my school days. To my school *St. Patrick's Girl's High School*. To the teachers of my school who loved me. To all the things that made me and to all the things that shattered me.

To my younger brother who stood by my side never letting me stumble and shiver; to those little hands which had wiped my tears. To my elder brother who helped me through it. To my parents, mamma and papa, who despite my differences had never stopped me from writing. To my group of seven friends whom we call Baby Shark. To my twin. To my cousins who had understood my pain and stood with me in the protests. To my late grandmother who would quote ancient stories resting in her bosom to me. To my late grandfather whose dictionary taught me a great diversity of English vocabulary. To my cats who would sit on my laps purring as I write.

To all the authors whose books I have read, especially to Enid Blyton whose writings inspired me to start writing at the age of nine. To everyone I had met whose bodies and eyes told stories of clouds to me.

To everyone I had forgotten to mention.

To the small yet vivid universes outside me; to the small yet vivid universes inside me. In the end to *Al-Khaaliq* the Creator of those small yet vivid universes both outside me and inside me.

PREFACE:

Before we begin this journey,

This book is a collection of all the thoughts that made me sleep and that kept me awake. It is about the sun and the moon. It is about everything the universe had offered me. It is about me. And maybe somewhere about you.

The collection contains twelve parts, each dealing with a particular topic of poetry. From *the reigns of antiquity* to *end*. Every part begins and ends with a story, either of my imagination or story I have witnessed through my naked eyes. These are the events that unfolded right in front of me making me write poetries after poetries.

These are all the questions I have asked myself and all the answers my pen gave me. These are all the stars that had fallen and stars that still shine. This book is the path I paved for myself to rummage myself in it. It is my love for nature and Karachi and an attempt to cure it. It is my pain of choosing some wrong paths.

I hope you find yourself in these pages or at least the ways to find yourself. I hope my words live in your bosom just as they have lived in me. For with each word I had hoped to adorn the lands with this asset of mine

As you leave for the journey, I'll just say, *'Good luck readers. Have a safe journey through my fallen stars'*

BOOK ONE: The Reigns of Antiquity

INTAMINATIS FULGET HONORIBUS

Untarnished, she shines with honor

Stars in the Night Sky

The album was closed. She did not close it. It closed itself.

She could not stare at the pictures anymore. For pictures bring memories and memories are sacred. Sacred things are heavy. They have braids of emotions hanging on them. And even if the pictures speak pleasures, the memories bring loss. So, the album closed itself on Anna's lap.

She glanced at the breaking of dawn. Sighed. For the world never ceases its motion even if millions of rhythms are dying every day. And it was her big day. The entrance examination for the field of military. A woman of Karachi stood under the tangerine aurora praying, as the cockerel in her garth crowed, to serve the lands of Pakistan.

She dressed herself and stood beside the large window waiting for her father to finish his breakfast. It was when her eyes caught hold of a familiar skin, familiar eyes, she glared at her reflection in the window. Started hearing all those voices as she looked deeper and deeper; her brother saying *you have the round eyes of baji*[1]. Her father saying *you are as beautiful as your mother.* Her uncle saying *you are as resilient as your grandmother.* Her friends saying *you are as wise as the generations of women in your family.* Her own voice saying *one day you will be a soldier like your grandfather.* And all those voices made her see inside her all those she had lost to mud. Her own reflection became a constellation of her

---

[1] An Urdu word to refer to an elder girl especially one's elder sister.

histories. Beholding herself, she saw that her ancestors were not gone, but they had wrapped themselves around her skin and soul. Looking at herself she realized she would never need the album anymore.

And that's what histories do, they tether to you like stars tether to the night sky, making you pleasant to look at, making you beautiful.

I wear my histories

Like a bird wears her feather

Stories of generations

Living in me

Like a life living in death

Blood of my forefathers

And breathes of matriarchs of my ancestry

Their skins have not decayed

They have wrapped themselves around me

I carry them

Like the sea carry waves

With all the colors and colorless voids

I wear them like a queen's gown

For the tragedies of my blood

Swirl above me, I wear them as a crown.

- (Histories)

Years after years went by, no festival seemed like before

When you were there to give me the goodwill Eidi[2] a little more.

And rise up earlier than any of us, on Eid's dawn

I had been always the first one you kissed as the day was born.

Covered in new clothes while shivered your old hands

Carried your stick, your legs too weak to stand.

Years after years went by, no Eid and Ramadan seemed like before.

When we have you in amongst us, no more.

And even when I sat beside you in days and nights

How you told me you want to see my marriage

And play with my children and watch them grow

In that place you both are now

I wish you behold it from the clouds

That even if there was no way to immortalize you

I turned your memories into words

And your histories into worlds

---

[2] A present given to younger people of the family, usually in the form of money, on Eid.

When even my father didn't know what I wish to eat

You, *Dada* used to stroll stumbling in the roads

To get me my favorite jellies

When even my mother used to yell at me

You, *Dadi* was my only shield to set me free.

In between you both, little Aimen used to sleep.

A dozen grandchildren you had

But it was me who was blessed to grow

Within your embrace

It was the most beautiful to me;

Your wrinkled face.

That I never thought this jewel would go away

As sands from my hands

I kept it beneath my ribs, the loss I couldn't withstand.

But death pays no pity; it arrived and I lost you

To the skies,

To the mud,

To the clouds of heavens.

It was hard to see your eyes closed

It was hard to see your hands not shivering anymore

It was hard to see the sudden cease of motions

Which were rhythm to my daily songs

It was hard but it was there in front of me

You. *Dada. Dadi*

Wrapped in white. Eyes closed

Not listening to me anymore.

I tried to keep you with me

But it looked like, enough protection I did not endow

I lost you

And…

I don't eat those jellies now

- (Something Lost)

My brother once told me

To remain with the past

Not to linger on it

But remain in it

As a broken shard

I have traveled roads thinking

Maybe it was to mark myself

In histories

An obituary on graveyards

To be there in the gone

And so, I left a part of me behind

Growing out of that left shell

So, every part in me still aches

As some still burn in past hell.

- (Past Hell)

Wasn't it you, my elders?

Who told me to dismiss

All those annoying guests,

Saying you weren't at home

While you were there.

So, I know now the art of deception

Wasn't it you my elders?

Who asked me to fear away

The little kittens on your couch

So that they don't shit

On your expensive 'sofas'.

So, I know now how to haunt

And fear away the weaker

Wasn't it you my elders?

Who told me to best

The neighboring child,

And be like all those

You perceived idols

With such luxurious fate.

So, now I know how to

Imitate.

Wasn't it you my elders?

Who taught me how

Important is the letter *A*

On my grade paper

And how abasing

The letter *F* is

So now I am revolted

By the failures knowing that they have tried.

Now, all those with that letter F

I can't help but deride.

Wasn't it you my elders?

Who dictated your decisions

To me.

Never sparing me

The chance.

Now whatever dilemma comes to me

I don't know the art of how to decide

But now when I am practicing

Lie, vanity and hate

Why do you abhor me?

When it was you who taught me each and every trait?

- (Wasn't it You, My Elders?)

If I have a child;

I will tell her

All the tales of my faults,

I will make her believe

It is okay to make mistakes

To get the identity of being human;

To get the mark of growth

If I have a child;

Even when no one does

I will put my faith

On her dreams and aims,

Which may look stupid to you

But if she says,

Momma, I want to touch the clouds.

I will tell her that she can

Build ladders to the sky,

And erect palace's wall on the clouds.

I will tell her *Don't worry about anyone else*

When all you have to do is make yourself proud

For when the wishes come to you

Within your reach arrives every cloud.

If I have a child;

I will teach her the silliest things,

Make her feel like a fairy

With majestic yet hidden wings

Which can fly

To the depths of the sky.

And if anyone makes a guffaw,

If anyone jeers

I will tell her you are exactly where you need to be

If you love, just stay.

Never be least pushed

By what the people have to say

For not they have ventured into the depths of your bones

Never seen the visions

Of your imagined thrones.

If I have a child;

I will make her feed the kittens on the street,

And the dogs and donkeys

A share of her own treat.

I will endow her

with that coup

Which grants that unnamed feel

That comes when you heal

Ones with no words to speak.

I will show her the good

In befriending the weak.

If I have a child;

I will respect her fear,

I will respect the unnamed phobias.

Her distance from the world.

I will never tell her to be brave

Or to be 'social'

Because it had never worked.

I will tell her how to accept what she is

With all the vulnerable part,

And weaknesses

And to love all what others find hideous

Because she is exactly what she needs to be

Exactly captured, enough free.

I will tell her don't be what people seek

It's okay to have scars,

And definitely fine to be weak

If I have a child;

I will love what she loves

And if I can't, then I will try not to hate

What her bodies emanate.

I will tell her there is nothing she lacks.

I will teach her how to fight back,

Yet how to forgive but not forget

Cause ones with the guns

Love the taste of giving threats.

If I have a child;

I will not forget what it was to be one

Finding stars even when the sky

Has a sun.

And I have given it the shape of ink

So, when I have a child;

I don't forget my word,

I am not least beguiled.

Only if I have a child;

I will never tame

What was meant to be wild.

- (If I Have a Child)

Stories of the Stars.

Anna laid injured on the hospital bed. Her daughter standing at the bed's foot. Anna smiled at her weeping girl. She had no strength left to utter a word but she knew like herself one day her daughter too will realize that Anna had not gone anywhere but her mother had just wrapped herself on her daughter's skin. Anna knew that her daughter will find her mother in her own reflection someday. For Anna knew the truth only seldom know: *No one dies, they just start living in other bodies*

Maybe she would be what Anna was, or maybe she would play a story the generations of Akbar had never played. Either way, she would carry histories as jewels around her neck. The past festooning her bosom.

For even the stars shine when they have stories of histories to tell.

BOOK TWO: Trials and Appraisals

IGNIS AURUM PROBAT

Fire tests gold

The Beauty of Fires

The smoke-filled her lungs, her room and even her heart. All these days she had curtailed herself from this mercy. She pulled the cigarette gently from her lips, her fragile fingers swerving. She inhaled the smoke again as one dying inhales oxygen. It was not a custom in the East to accept the smoke leaving a girl's lips. Girls curtail themselves of this ailment, less to save their lungs more to save their respect in the eyes of society. Fortunately, or unfortunately, Sarah was not one of them for it was already enough ruined; both her lungs and her respect.

There was a knock on the door. Sarah inhaled and exhaled. A knock again.

'Come out, Sarah', her mother called as a thunderstorm striking the walls

'What do you want?' Sarah called from her bed, half her voice disappearing beneath the pain and the smoke in her ribs.

'Just open the door', a calm reply followed.

Sarah tucked the cigarette in between her lips and made her way to the door without cleaning her smeared mascara.

Her mother sighed as her eyes paused at the cigarette but she said not a word. 'He is a good man, Sarah, and he is your husband after all.'

Sarah let more tears fall. 'And what are these?' she said pointing to all the patterns of colors caged in all the canvases. 'My sweat, my pain, my cries, my nights I have spent working on them. All of them, they are my twenty years'

'Listen…' her mother tried to speak

'I trusted you, ma.', she wiped her cheek, the mascara being carried by her palm, 'I gave you all the keys and now when I am locked you won't come to let me out' Sarah said with a limp in her voice, a stumble in her lips. The cigarette fell from her lips, the smoke churning as waves to the ceiling

'There is no way out', her mother said with gritted teeth

'There is'

She picked the cigarette and tucked it again between her lips

'He is rich, he is famous. He rules over the country. He can give you anything you want' her mother said

Sarah smirked through the corner of her lips 'Not *everything* I want'

Sarah stared at her mother's tears hidden behind her lids. She knew it would kill her mother if she leaves her hell, but it would kill her if she stays in that hell for only she could see the flames obscured by curtains of diamonds and golds. Only she was burning in it.

The black thick smoke

Spewing out from the gap of jaws,

Churning into the throat.

It kills.

It heals.

A pill.

A feel.

The liquor of haze

Swallowing into the lungs.

The known toxic.

The known killer.

The known aid.

The known addiction

To the known taste.

What is in that poison?

What is so mystical?

For it rules over lungs

That devour it,

To ultimately devour them.

Abased as a source of disease

Facing revulsion and hate;

While just curtailing

The long, torturous path to fate.

It's hated, it's adored.

Some not willing to lose it,

Some not willing to gain,

As for some, it devours the lungs.

For some, it devours the pain.

- (It Kills; It Heals)

The hell, they say,

Is a place they fear

Full of demons residing

And flames burning there.

They never felt or saw,

The place that exists

Behind the invisible mists.

But He put me in a place,

Where I felt a demonic death.

Yet breathing.

He put me to introduce

To let me know how it feels,

To be burning within the flames

Which do not exist.

Yet I choke and turn to ashes,

When its name I hear.

He let me in

To let me know the fear.

Even though that hell be covered in

Visible blankets of diamond,

But what they didn't see;

Are that invisible curtains of mist,

Behind which the demons exist,

And the fire ignites.

So, that I can know and understand

Why I don't and why I can't

Belong to these flames veiled in crystals,

And so away I can rise

To my paradise.

Away from this hell.

Away from these walls.

From these choking anxieties,

And useless boundaries.

Maybe on my way to Eden

I'd meet death,

But death marks the end of pain,

And hell was the beginning of it.

He put me in hell.

He put me in it

To make me realize

"O lady, here, you don't fit".

When you turn to ashes,

Even when they see no flame.

Argue not.

Turn to ashes,

But then be carried away,

To the abode of joie de vivre.

- (The Fire behind the Crystals)

What's greater example of my love I can tell;

I gave you the keys to unlock my hell.

And now when the hell is locked

With me burning inside, aching with the breeze.

The people I love, to whom I handed over the keys

Won't even come and save me from the flame.

While burning, I am still calling out their name.

- (Keys of the Hell)

I rolled again in my bed, oh, it was night again.

The moon was up, the lights went off, and here comes the pain.

I closed my eyes, but the chaos was awakened by the moon.

Haunting my peace for the rest of the night.

The chaos inside,

Had my sleep died.

I sat up in my bed, inhaling so deep.

But alas again it won, crushing me.

My healed wounds started to seep.

My bones murmur melancholy in the air,

I fell again into the void of my fear.

But I knew with the sun's gold

Every thought will vamoose.

For the moon likes my taste. I am only its prey.

So, I laid down again watching as moved the clock's hand.

There'll be sun so soon.

I closed my eyes but many pictures came rolling in;

Pictures of the past and fears and the scars on my skin.

As I was rolling in the sheet, my sweat mixed with my tears,

My mind was playing a script of everything my soul fears.

Believe me, it's scary, it's really insane

Crying the whole night, and then welcoming the sun again.

So, as the sunlight pierces in,

And touches my skin.

I had to get up from the bed.

When away, to the unseen skies, the moon goes.

The pain.

The memories; my heart swallows.

(Scary Night)

The smell of perfume emanating

From those colorful beads,

Which you have named as Flowers.

And oh, their sight is such tantalizing

As the sun reflects on the petals clear.

The flames in our bodies touch our skins.

The death of petals starts being born.

For a moment, the victim forgets

The endowment of petals with a thorn.

And as he touches it,

For the temptation that comes with beauty is

Irresistible.

Pulse throbs in his veins.

And blood pours out.

Here the sight of paradise betrays him.

Agony arrives.

So, when even the sounds and sights,

Feels like a sun covering the nights.

Recall all the flowers and the garden.

Remember, folks

There could be hymns,

The devil sings.

And deceit in the stories

The angel has to tell.

There are hells in heaven

And heavens in hell

- (Heavens in Hells)

What do you call it?

Pain? Agony? Anguish?

What do you call it people?

When bones go crashing to the floor,

When your weight is melting away;

But you still feel heavy.

I don't call it pain.

It's colossal than just four letters.

I don't call it agony

It melts like ice,

And burns as fire.

Pain fills you

But it? It leaves a void,

An abyss.

With no walls and roofs,

Yet suffocating.

What do you call it, people?

For it is not pain, not anguish.

Pain can be turned into poetries.

And it? It is when my ink gets dried,

And paper all empty.

It is not even death,

For death is confinement in the mud.

It has no name, I guess.

When it comes, it doesn't confine me.

When it comes, it feels like

In a bottomless pit, I fell.

It is those ice which makes

The blazing fire in hell.

- (Nameless)

The waves of cloud cascading.

A tide of thunders.

A smoke of sand.

All tangling like iron chains around

My neck covered in braiding stains.

I am obscured by a shroud of arsenals

With weapons to kill me instead

For the best way to save someone

The best way is to render them dead.

- (The Best Way)

Kindled a candle for the flame to blow.

But the poor candle becoming slow.

It was young, the wax looked enough,

But only the candle knew how the air was rough.

For its flame flickered as the air blows.

Young candle slowing down as no time goes.

A little more air can kill the flame.

No matter how hard the candle tries

The flame will extinguish.

But even without the flame, the candle has to live,

The wax is still left there.

Doesn't matter every time its flame is killed by the air

The candle is us, its wax our life, its flame our smile

Air, is the people around, which makes the flame fragile.

Even though when flame is gone, the air had done its theft,

The candle has to live as the wax is still left.

So even when the smile is gone, people had done their theft.

We still have to survive as wax, our life, is still left.

- (The Poor Candle)

This is a poem about the moon as it looked over me while I talked to you.

This is a poem about the birds that chirped at the dawn to wake me up beside you.

This is a poem about the roses that have been wilting in the vases since you have given them to me.

This is a poem about the dewdrops that fell on our skins.

This is a poem about the roads that must be traveled to reach you.

This is a poem about the world that makes both of us rotate the sun at the same time.

This is a poem about the clouds I sent to you.

This is a poem about the words I left at your door.

This is a poem about the door you closed at my face.

This is a poem about the pictures of us the walls of my house embrace.

This is a poem about my heart as it broke under your reign.

This is a poem about us wrapping ourselves together just to let go one day.

This is a poem of all your broken promises to stay

This is a poem not about you…

This is a poem about me... about how *I* let you mute every song.

This is a poem about how I let myself be deceived by a touch, so wrong.

This is a poem about how I weaken myself to let you become strong.

This is not a poem…

This is an obituary about our love that died.

This is a grave when my red ink dried.

- (This is a)

Darkness Makes Stars.

'Isn't he your ex-husband?' Ahmad whispered in her ears.

At first, Sarah could not believe her eyes but slowly as reality poured into her mind, she nodded. It was him with a little girl by his side wearing a frock of abstract patterns and eyes as round as his. She jumped her way towards Sarah.

'I love you' the girl announced to Sarah. Despite her face bearing marks of his, Sarah could not help but smile at the little voice.

'Who are you, kid?' Sarah said bowing down to face the girl

'I am Maria' the girl said pulling out her hand

Sarah shook her hands, 'I am Sarah'

The girl waves her hands in the air, 'Oh I know you.' She smiled just the smile of the man standing behind her. 'I want to be in your art school one day' she said. At those words Sarah's chest swelled more, her smile widened like a crescent on the sky. 'Who is he?' she said eyeing to him

The girl turned, 'My Papa' she said waving to the man.

Sarah stared at him and then to the colossal tower of her school standing behind her. Her heart beating with the pulse of victory in her veins.

Ahmad handed the girl a painting by Sarah 'It's for you, Maria' he said, 'We will be waiting for you to join our school' he patted the girl on her head and she leaped into a hug.

Hours after the girl had gone, Sarah sat on her school's door. Ahmad beside her. 'He has a daughter…' Sarah said.

'You will have one too, Sarah' Ahmad said gazing at the night sky above them

'No, Ahmad. He has a daughter who wants to be in *my* art school. The art school whose mere idea he used to hate so much' Sarah said.

Ahmad glances at her, the moon reflecting in his eyes and in his smile. 'You are the women some men fear, and some dare to love'

Sarah smiled briefly, 'Only cigarettes and colors dare to love me'

Ahmad held out a cigarette wrapped in a ribbon, 'Will you smoke with me till the colors live on the earth?' he said, his blue eyes shining under the dark sky and smile turning to delighted chortle. He looked deep into her eyes; his palm held out.

Sarah took the cigarette smiling. Ahmad took a deep breath of smoke that formed a mist against the star covered night. She gazed at him and the waves of smokes leaving his lips, she gazed at the huge towers of the art school behind her, and she gazed at the stars. If she had never left her former husband, if she had feared the risk of darkness, she would have never been a star.

'I will', Sarah said exhaling airs of smoke in synchrony with the man sitting beside her in clothes drenched in her colors and lungs in her smoke.

BOOK THREE: The Pouring Aspersion

ILLEGITIMI NON CARBORUNDUM

Don't let the bastards get you down

The Different Stars.

'No five fingers are equal', Maida said under her breath yet her father heard it

'You have to make them equal' he said and slammed the door behind him.

Maida let her weight fall on the torn piles of pages. Each page torn at the edges and filled with scribbles of frustration. There were even pages on which no words were able to be deciphered. Maida took another handful of pages and tore them with not the slightest touch of pity passing through her. The coziness of her pillow opened its wide arms around Maida's head and, slowly releasing the crumpled torn piece, she glared at her long slender fingers drenched in black ink. Her nails had edges bitten bluntly by her teeth and her skin soaked in the scratches of her nails. She glanced at the long slender unequal fingers. The thumb was the smallest of all yet how ironic, it seemed to her, the thumb wears the crown of strength. Its dwarfism being balanced on the scale

You have to make them equal. The words of her father drummed echoes around her. And so, she pulled, with all her mighty force she tried to pull the thumb up to the level of her longest finger, she failed.

She gazed too long at her hand thinking, why in the same hand Allah had given different fingers? Why in the same world had He given different people? Different yet equal. For like the thumb, the scales were always balanced

The curiosity grew such mammoth in her that she tossed her Mathematics book away and grabbed an empty paper sketching out a hand with fingers of the same anatomy. And therein her art, she found the answer. We are all different to make the world beautiful.

Everyone cannot be an engineer, but everyone cannot be an artist too.

She looked at her doodles on the walls and all the abstract aestheticism the cover of her book is laden with. And then she spared a glimpse on her result card and the queue of F.

'What will the people say? A daughter of a professor is failing again and again? What will the people say? My daughter is so dumb? What will the people say? You have such dark circles under your eyes, what will the people say? All these mashups of dried paints on your hands make it such hideous. What will the people say if you do not pass? What will the people say?

People's tongues have straddled our hands suffocating it out of its blood. People's tongues are the same ropes that will kill us. But death is inevitable, right? So why worry about what rope will come to strangle your neck?

Maida glanced at the vesper sky. No sun and no stars. Then she found one. A little small. She found another much larger. And another at a greater distance. And another with a dim light.

Different stars make beautiful nights.

Hitherto the entity of time

Carries no element of wait.

Forgiven is the crime

The criminal is endowed with hate.

The crawling then carries a cane,

All the colossal towers

Become mundane.

You cannot decipher the augur

That comes with aurora;

And then speak of how melancholic

Suddenness creates your fate.

Even though you do illiterate.

If your heart carries no faith

Or your vision is obscured by mist,

Means not the truth does not exist.

- (Truth)

I am done keeping quiet,

Done following every rule.

Why do I have to be silent?

I am done being a fool.

I bowed to every careening behest

That I left behind what was of me the best.

Regulations of silence,

I was expected to abide by

I wasn't given any right to defy.

But I am done with it.

I now identify

My own existence a sui generis of nature.

My flaws, my idiosyncrasies

My perfections, my infinities

They are all mine to take.

Order not, I only take advices

My decisions are mine to make.

I know the open lies I hold,

And hidden truths I never told.

You know less or you know not of me.

You don't know what I cannot,

And what I can best be.

I am done reflecting through your mirror.

I am done being sculpted by your hands.

I want to cultivate myself on my very own lands.

I was a fool of making sandcastle of my dreams,

You were ruining it, lesser was it able to withstand.

But I am done with it, you can't break it more,

For I have rendered my dreams into scattered sand.

Your pursuits; I do respect

But I have my own path, I can't neglect.

The path only I can and have to protect.

I don't know how to stop

The restlessness when I rest

- (I am Done)

Bow down to their throne?

Why?

I have my own to sit on.

My own lands to rule upon.

Why their law should I follow?

When there is nothing of them

That I know.

They are all strangers to me.

How can I amend myself?

Into something they want me to be.

"Don't do it", you say

For you fear

"Log kya kahengy?"

But must I surrender

In front of their tongues?

Am I that feeble?

I am the strength of a young,

I have made my own Kingdom.

And I have my own laws.

Where I shouldn't care,

What they think of my flaws.

"Log kya kahengy"[3]

Cannot make my dreams depart:

Depart my existence?

No, they are my part.

I won't put my weapons down.

I won't bow to their crown.

When I have my own jewels to wear,

And diamonds to be festooned with.

I am stronger, I don't fear.

They can't ruin my reign,

And the lands I own.

For like a Griffin

I am strong to handle my throne.

They may emit fire,

So that I can burn

And from my persistent self

Into ashes, I would turn.

But I don't fear their burning despise

For like a Phoenix

---

[3] A phrase used a lot in the Eastern countries to eat away a dreamer's freedom. "What will the people say?" (in Urdu language)

From ashes, again I shall rise.

- (Log Kya Kahengy?)

Layers after layers, I added on my skin;

A process possessing antiquity.

Some layers drenched in colors,

Some layers made of curves.

Layers after layers, I added on my skin.

Just to please you.

All of you

I was ugly with a shade of dark caramel

So, I added the cream of porcelain.

I had bags under my eyes

So, I added lashes that weren't mine.

I was a girl of the darkest corners

So, I festooned my walls with alleys of people.

I had no geometry from my eyes to soles

So, I carved out edges.

I had a nose buried in books

So, I put a golden ring on my nose.

My lips were a color of clouds

So, I added layers of twilight skies.

Layers after layers, I added on myself.

While me? I grew thinner and thinner

My reality was so weak to collapse down.

For I was afraid what if you saw

The hideous core.

Would you even want me anymore?

I was afraid to be left alone,

In a world where people make the throne.

But I never knew every layer of ice meltdown;

Every layer except your blazing gown,

Which you are deep beneath

Right amid your core,

So, the layers did. They melted.

Each time unfolding to unravel me.

I was weakening.

For I thought, I was a duckling

Made to follow the queue in the lakes.

What I did not know was that;

I am an eagle made of feathers that never flake.

An eagle who wears the crown;

Solitary.

An eagle who is the highest on the skies

Above the clouds;

Solitary.

The air traipses down to my core,

Wanting it more and more.

Layers after layers melted.

And I came to know myself!

It takes ages,

To make or to break

the cages.

- (Layers)

Break the cages which surround us,

We all breathe the same air around us.

The cages built by race, money, and cast

The Creation of the same God,

These cages separate.

The soft walls of the heart

Are being hardened by hate.

We are may be all built on different architectures,

But the same bricks were used to create you and me.

We may have different rooms,

But they are under the same sky.

Oh, who fears water?

When as drops, it is separated,

But when they come together

A mighty sea is created.

Like a rope

Strengthened by its every strand.

We should stand

Shoulder to shoulder,

Hand in hand.

In this colossal Earth,

My screams are turned to whispers

But if together we speak

Our whisper can turn into a scream;

The power of amalgamation,

How could we blaspheme?

In this puzzle of Earth, we are the pieces.

We may be different and totally opposite,

But it's only when we come together

We can fit.

We can solve it.

There is no other way around,

Only if in synchrony we march

The air will echo with our footstep's sound.

We may have different darkness,

But we have the same Sun.

We may have different names,

But we are all known as *'Human'*.

- (Together)

Call me what you want.

And say me what you can.

While you're busy hating me,

I'll finish what I began.

Come cut me, pierce me

Make your knives go deep.

Pick a sharper than the sharpest breed.

Cut me, I'll feed my paper

With words, I'll bleed.

There is no dream that can ever rot.

Not a single thing, a human cannot.

Chase me away.

Be the predator, I the prey.

But forget not,

A lion cannot run as fast as a deer,

I'll run with a speed:

Not even ignis fatuus can bear.

I'll take the speed of light.

Illuminate I will.

Call me trivial or careless.

Anything as you may.

Speak, say all you want to say.

I'll make your words, weapon mine to use,

And cherish my readers with a joy of abuse.

You say my will have to die,

And it's useless even if I try.

But forget not,

When you sleep soundly,

Or go dancing at night,

My hands keep working

I just write, write and write.

And when comes out the sun,

You begin

While I'm done.

What can haters do?

Except to hate?

It's not your tongue,

But my hands that carry my fate.

- (Haters)

Every day I am ordered to learn,

Learn skills for which I wasn't born.

Every day I must educate,

And dive into the pages I hate.

They live in a prejudice

That this degree will make me fly.

Every day these books kill me

Was I born to everyday die?

A constant and so eternal

A battlefield is education.

Where you stand with weapons,

Your mind can't bear.

And fight against your own nation.

Where your own parents push you

To stand ahead in the queue,

And keep standing there.

Even though that place makes you feel lost,

Even though chasing good grades

Makes you exhaust.

I hope when we grow up,

Never do we forget

Learning to get good grades

Is the worst mindset.

Don't quit learning.

Don't learn to earn.

Not even for fame.

Don't settle in a battle,

Learn what you're born for.

A bird can't learn how to swim,

The bird is educated to spread its wings.

If she quits learning how to fly,

She can never leave the nest.

Learn, what you're born for

Don't learn to get the best.

Learn what you love to do

Learn what makes you *"you"*.

- (A Battle of Education)

The world is but an abattoir.

The blood of dreams churning

Is what the people devour.

And quietly millions of owners,

Of millions of dreams,

Let it be slaughtered.

So, who was the murderer here?

Who was the betrayer?

And now it's my turn.

A sharp blade, a bottle of venom;

All weapons set on their tongues,

All the mountains falling on me.

A storm careening.

But I won't let my silence

Engulf my dreams, my chest.

All eyebrows raising as I smile;

There was no fret on my face,

No worries, no sadness, no grimace.

In this moment of defeat

The uninvited victory I feel.

I've taught my dreams hard

How from their venom, it should heal.

For when their weapons

Become your strength,

And your courage

Their vulnerabilities.

You may not always avail victories,

But always you'll come back

Undefeated...

They can start a war.

And get their armed army on the field

But my dreams cannot be shattered.

And the world's permission

Had never really mattered.

Let the storm come in,

Let the earth tear apart,

Call the waves,

Let the massacre flow.

I'll still reach to the place

I have always longed to go.

- (Abattoir)

The dusk came

Lost all its hues, the sky

The demons were set free.

Black wings began to fly.

I hid in a corner

So afraid of the storm.

The agony mixed with air,

Rushed in each lung.

The memories vanished with a thwack

The pictures fall off, which once hung.

The night was there,

The gray branches bare·

The echoing howl.

Replenishing my fear.

I swerve, I cry.

When will this be gone away?

My every breath was going astray.

My body cringed

When will this vanish and disappear?

Cosmic strength,

But unable to any longer bear.

I could die or try

How longer will I hide?

Shivering, I still tried.

I stood and fell of the dark around,

But I stood again, I need the light to be found.

Suddenly then through the eastern windows

Hied towards the dark room, a light.

I was able to stand up

It kept returning my sight.

The colors were all back again

The trees weren't any more mundane.

My lips got the energy

To work against gravity

So then smiled I.

My bosom exploded

At the brightness of the sky.

It was all changing, I don't know how

As if a wand had been twirled

Magic on Earth, did God allow?

But then sooner or later, realized I

To return again,

My happiness needed me to try.

Behind all that mess,

Kept waiting for me;

Was my happiness.

- (The Return of Happiness)

The smile on your face

It's worth every praise

An artist's work is to which you allude

It's unbelievable, your pulchritude.

With every scar and stain

And with every smell, your sweat can create

An aura of success, you radiate,

And every scar is not a flaw

In it, your history is concealed

Telling stories of how

Your wounds were healed.

You rise and you fall

But you are still a star.

You rush and destruct

A williwaw you are.

Care not what the people say

Let their words wander

In the air without an aim.

Stick to what you call yourself

Stick to your own name.

Smile, love

Never shall I abandon you

You'll see me right in front of the mirror

Whatever you are going through

You'll see me

Looking back at you.

My mere reflection, you are not

You are all the lessons I was taught.

You are all the fights I have fought.

You are all the dreams that I caught.

In this eerie blandness of universe

You are the only star, you are the sun

In this world that lacks magic

You are me, you are Aim-MON.

Protect me, protect you, love.

You are the picture on the mirror

That is always enough.

- (Picture on the Mirror)

Who are you without your voice?

Who are you without the bosom that explodes?

Who are you without the treasury of scars?

Who are you without your dark?

Who are you without your stars?

Who are you without which that echoes in you?

Who are you without which that flows in you?

Who are you without your fall?

Who are you without your rise?

Who are you without your dreams?

Who are you without your fate?

Who are you without everything in you they abominate?

Who are you without every book you read?

Who are you without every song you sing?

Without each of it, you are a mere….

…nothing

- (Who Are You?)

Are you tired, little life?

Then go, take a break.

A complete pause

From every engagement around

A complete quietness

To listen to your own breath's sound.

Are you tired, little life?

Oh, stop running now

For even if you come back later

You'll run again somehow.

The water of oceans takes rest too

Even if for a while, stagnant is what they be

Never can it make them less deadly.

Oh, see the ferocious bears around

For months they'd go hibernate

But when they come back

Some life, under their jaws, would suffocate.

Are you tired, little life?

Go be inert for a while,

Rest in your chrysalis

Pause all the busy things

So, when the chrysalis breaks

You come back with wings.

Are you tired, little life?

Being torpid for a while,

Inactivity is not bad, little life

You seem tired.

Go, take a break

The fainéant period is for you, little life.

A moment of nature,

An autumn of rest,

When the burdens of leaves are left

So, the trees get prepared for the arrival of springs

A time for you to develop your wings.

- (Are You Tired?)

How much should I care?

I strolled through the roads of thorn

With my feet, all bare.

I want to run on the oceans

With soft water beneath my soles.

I want to live my youth

And not waste it chasing their goals.

I want a cloud to come carry me

Above the busy roads

So, I can touch the sky

And let go of the burdens and loads.

I want to roll on the sand.

I want the rose to fill my lungs

With its aroma.

I want to sit high on a mountain

To behold the aurora.

I want to climb the Everest

And cuddle with its snow

I want to climb so high

And forget about the 'below'.

I want to write many stories

And poems touching infinities.

I want to touch the bodies

Of all the galaxies.

I want to collect all the stars

From the sky, that had fallen.

I want to live my life,

This busy world had stolen.

- (I Want to)

Let me just speak the truth:

The world is not for you

It won't embrace

Or caress your wounds

Rather

It will suck your blood

Like a man at a desert, drink.

Aim your weapons now

Or weapons would be aimed at you.

Their gentle smile is faux

What is not visible, is true.

Do them no harm, my dear

But in no way

Let them harm you.

Don't look down

If your eyes make them squint

When they have other ways to look too.

Do them no harm

And let them not harm you.

- (Let Them Not Harm You)

It was supposed to be my asset

Only my pendant to wear

A medallion to embellish

The days this planet has me to bear.

This life was mine to live,

This body mine to shape,

It was mine to decide

What servitude to it I should give

I can do whatever with it

This life is mine to live.

I need not be my version of you

It's my loss or my success

My life is not yours to mess.

You dare not speak.

And dare not dream

Of what I should be.

It's my turn to breathe

To be a me-er version of me.

And I am not sorry,

That I can't fit into your mold

I am not sorry,

That I am a williwaw, made not to be controlled.

- (A Protest)

You open your arms to die;

Have you forgotten?

You can move your wings to fly.

Life isn't stern and so isn't death.

You can either hold your

Or hold *onto* your breath.

It gives you a chance to inhale again

The pure mist around.

It gives you a chance to change.

Death doesn't come when wanted

Because no nature

Takes its creature

For granted.

Nature, as merciful as it is

Has blessed us with a strength

To live with weaknesses.

But will you be able to live with it

When it is something you despise?

Wings are the weakest part of a bird

But through this weakness, it flies.

You may feel lonely, but you are not

You have yourself

You can get the battle fought.

Every worst battle you can subdue

When with you, for you

Loving you is *"you"*.

- (You)

All the voices surround me

When they announce my failure,

Speak my abasement,

Words repeating my past.

When I look at the people,

Rummaging through their eyes

To find a glint of

A mere strand of

Hope

I find none.

They have no hope in me

No faith.

My heart just sinks down

My veins enmesh

Dryness of my lips making voices

when I bite them to bleed.

They scrutinize me

As a mannequin.

An abortive mannequin.

I used to fear them

I used to let them drink me

I used to stay under the rose

I tried to work behind the doors.

A fool I was,

I wanted so bad what was *theirs*

It was *their* hope

Their faith

Their defined success

Their respect

Their love

Their words of praise

I wanted it so bad

I forgot I have my orchard too

Where these roses bloom.

They can keep their own

I don't want it for God's sake,

I have my own to give

My own to take.

I took a handful of *my* faith

And gave it to myself

I gave a scintilla of *my* love to me.

When I got *my* love

I heard *my* voices speak to me

From their cages of success,

They wanted me free.

I took *my* moves

Made *my* aim

Worked *my* dreams

Inevitably *my* success came.

Screw it, *theirs* is not *mine*

Without *theirs,* I am more than just fine

With *mine*, I am more than even I

I put all *my* faith in me

I never lost *my* hope in me

I worked for *my* dreams

I got *my* aim

Don't want to be called a Shakespeare

I have *my* own name

And above all,

When I got *my* love

I never abraded *my* part they abhor

With all *mys,* me, I endow

So, I don't need even an atom of *theirs* now.

- (I Have *Mys* for Me)

It's okay if you just lay down on the bed

Who told you running will get you ahead?

All of the world is in this endless marathon

They run, just run with nowhere to go

You can stop right here,

Who told you to go with the flow?

It's okay if you don't have a dream

And you wander aimlessly

It's okay if all you do is breathe through

Sometimes that is the hardest thing to do

Life was not given to chase our preys

It was given to live our numbered days

Who said to all the time, of all the things, care?

It's okay if you just be here.

Your life has a purpose too,

Maybe you don't know

With every air you exhale

Your energies with the wind blow.

And the night shines, and the day is ablaze

For you are sharing your energy with the wind

And not on chasing your preys.

It's okay if you don't take stress

And your lips only smile

Your ecstasy gets in the wind

And nature gets agile.

So up come the flowers,

And the buds bloom

When with your energy swells the nature's bosom

And you become the next reason

How went away this year's barren autumn.

It's okay if you create your Utopia, your Arcady

And do nothing else

The nature fills with music

When in your Eden ring the bells.

Everyone has their own ways to give to the world

And it is your way to give

Everyone has their own ways to be happy,

And it is your way to live

Why like everyone else you should be filled with zeal?

It was your nothing that defines you

Nothing of you the world could steal

It's okay if you still have wounds to heal

It's okay, just be you

It's okay, do what you want to do

It's okay if there is nothing you did

It's okay, it was your energy

That made the world more vivid.

- (It is Okay)

I stood in the core of the damp walls

No exit to be seen

And slowly my lungs went tired

As the air turned into aqua

But I was not born with gills

And the universe seemed to

Know not about it.

The universe didn't give a damn

Of what it gave me

What it curtailed me of.

As the water mounted

To the skin beneath my nose

Just then a thought

Within me tiptoes.

At the moment when

Death seemed so close

It would sound crazy if I say

A thought of a spider

Came to me

A thought of vividness of the galaxy

Of never seen beauties

Never visited mysteries

Though there was no air around

But there was still some in me.

I emanated my air into the water

Trapping my own oxygen

In a bubble

Just large enough to carry my face

Just large enough to let me breathe.

My own air encapsulated in a sheath

Just like a diving bell

Letting me live

And as the bubble rose

It carried me to surface

Where the waves abut the air

Where life was so near

I survived, and now I am living

To tell you my tale

That even if you feel you are curtailed

Even when the air around you vanishes

And your lung famishes

Emit your own air from within the gaps of your bone

Let your air out just to breathe it in.

Inhale yourself

When there is nothing to breathe in around.

Just the way in the ghastly hush of night

You can still hear your own sound.

- (You're Air to Breathe)

The Scales Are Balanced.

Nineteen different countries. Her painted pictures had reached the homes of nineteen different countries across the globe. She gives meaning to shades. Life to art. She gives beauty to aches. She gives stars to the sky. She is the girl some people had called dumb, some fool, some by other names of derision. She is the same girl that carried the mark of failure on her wings. She is the one who couldn't pass the engineering examination.

She loves to stand on swords of their tongues. She loves to bleed. For blood is such pure red, it adds beauty to her painted roses. Maida, she is. The thumb. The smallest yet the king.

A girl who walks through Istanbul streets taking pictures of the sky is the same girl who failed three times in a row.

The world is a better place with those who turn emotions into colors and words. The world is beautiful for it is a rainbow of different colors. None the same but each equal for the scales are always balanced.

BOOK FOUR: "NATURE"

NATURA, ARTIS MAGISTRA

Nature, the mistress of art

Moons and Stars.

'Why is the night full of stars, mamma?' Amina asks. Her amber eyes like a pool of honey with golden twinkling stars floating on them. The bells of clock ringing in a distant room announcing the hands striking twelve.

Her mother smiles as her fingers move with agility knitting a sweater just the color of the sky above them.

'Why is the air so cold under the moon, mamma?' she asks again. Her hair dancing to the chilly winds caressing her cheeks and ears.

Her mother smiles, 'Did you perform your evening prayers, Amina?' she says

Amina nods still glaring at the night sky.

'Why do you think we pray *maghrib* when the sky is losing the sun and *fajr* when the sky is losing the stars?' her mother said.

Amina turns her gaze to her mother, 'Why?'

'It is the beauty of our *fajr* prayers that brings the Sun and its warmth. It is the charisma of our *maghrib* prayers that bring the stars and their chill just so the world can let go of the sun's fire and become a little cooler'

Years later a thirty years old Amina sits in the veranda of her little home, a beautiful cat purring beside her. The sky keeps turning darker. The same bells of the clock chiming in some distance. The cold winds caressing her cheeks. She looks at her mother's empty spot which is filled by the light of the moon. She inhales the moon's

air, the ripples of loneliness vanishing away as she stares
at the moon and the stars.

'I prayed for you to come' she says to the full moon
above them, 'I prayed for the midnight's air'.

Clear light to murk the winds turn

When the vesper sky loses its Sun.

But is brought the moon, by the evening's prayer

Is brought the moon by the midnight's air.

Let me breathe, for once

The midnight's air

The air which carries the dew drops

To dout the inferno that burns.

The flames of inferno;

Which makes:

The world seems unseen,

Which makes:

My vision stays unclear.

I want to inhale the midnight's air.

The drops of dew that have peace

So, vamoose the scintilla of despair.

I want to breathe the midnight's air

Dewdrops falling on my flames of agony

So evanesces every disturbance soon

When I fill my lungs under the midnight moon.

- (The Midnight's Air)

When lunar light, the sky shows

And all the eyes around close

When the wind silently flows

Comes to hum some poetries

And good prose

"Mr. The Heaven Knows".

You may not hear his voice

But it dries your pillows.

And puts your eyes to close

The wind changes at night

When away the sun goes

The wind changes at night

It gets tranquil.

Filling with his poetries and prose

Who is he? Nature doesn't disclose

"Mr. The Heaven Knows".

He wishes you good dreams

Under the rose.

You may never know him

But with a spell he cast

Vamooses the frown in your brows

Yes! The serenity in repose

Is brought by the magic of

"Mr. The Heaven Knows".

- (Mr. "The Heaven Knows")

On a wooden desk,

The candles burn

While the sphere queen of the night

Awaits the sun.

My door is open

In the servitude of fáilte

To the warm hush

Of the air outside

My windows are open;

My eyes glaring at the lights:

In the darkness, that hide.

The incense of old pages

Fills up each lung

I hum the ballads

That may never be sung.

But can serenity in reality last long?

As a creature as human steps in

The air jams with fracas's throng.

I close the door

To the voices:

Hath to be unheard.

And vamoose to non-existent

I close the windows

To the visions:

Must stay unseen.

And behold illusions.

Maybe the universe's reality

Was made to be escaped

Because the universe

Is filling with man and man-made.

- (Absconding Real)

Amidst all the wrong the world has done.

The Eastern sky never forgets

To bring up the Sun.

It sets down

But back it comes

With the sweet ballads

Every little bird hums.

The mammoth candle of the galaxy.

The only star of aurora's ataraxy.

The Eastern winds kindle the flame,

That blesses the world with some respite

For the sinners are awaken

By the hush of the night.

And when the sky loses its color

All the brethren must have gone blind

If there was nothing lunar at night

But the moon, too, reflects the sun's light.

We behold the universe;

From dusk to dusk

From dawn to dawn.

Our roof is no dark

Even when the sun is gone

For even when the sun is not there

Its light, to the sky, adhere.

But will the sun

For eternity burn?

Without its flame,

We'll suffer an insufferable loss

Darkness will settle deep

Into the void of the cosmos.

- (The sun)

Life: It is a rhythm

A sound, a music

The repetitions of inhales

And exhales.

A periodical arrival

Of smiles and ails.

With synchrony of motions

When our lips move

To quote our sacred notions.

And how it's both edges

In symmetry, curl up

Whenever we smile.

And our eyes follow

The same pattern of style.

They close together

And together their lids depart

But when it comes to music

Oh, listen to your heart.

Your soul moves to it

Your body lives through it.

It generates the power

It gives the heat.

Music is so appreciated by nature

Life is extant by a mere rhythm

Of heartbeat.

- (The Rhythm in Nature)

The winter winds come

Sunlight will not face revulsion anymore

The heat of flames will be embosomed

For here the winter winds come

Singing its ballads, reciting its hymn

Devouring its memorandum

To the leaves, to thy sweet wet skin.

The trees shall spew its leaves

And bless the land with hues of

Vermilion and tangerine pulchritude.

The winter winds kiss your cheek

Abrasive to touch

Thy sweet skin shall bow

And lose all its tan:

The provision of the sun.

Thy lips will split, bleed

Embracing the dry winter winds.

And then the clouds will rain snow

The branches all ready to carry it

And even the vast land below.

Somehow the cursed heat becomes divine

And is worshipped the inferno.

No ill-omen is the winter winds

Even though green dies,

Wound hurts,

Cold hollows the air

But there is this poetry

In the winter winds you can hear:

The rustling of leaves,

The land caressing it as it fall,

The seldom howls in the dark,

The whisper of the falling snow.

And it comes to let you know 'curse none'.

The extinguished flames are made again to burn.

Always avoided, now becomes

A divine blessing: the sun.

It shows the green will sure go away

It comes to let you know the gray

No evil it is,

If you just hear the words the winter winds say.

- (The Winter Winds)

Little tiny turfs of ball,

I am amazed

At the aestheticism of creation

Life can sing in the bodies

Such solely pure,

Such solely deeming as innocence,

For it is such an unusualness

Hearing the music of breath

From chirps and purrs

And woofs and many more

Many with no words to define them

At least not in our languages.

Such music whose meaning is a mystery

Still a solace in these loudening thunders.

When I see and hear and smell and touch

All the different colors, life can be in

All the different songs, life can sing

All the different fragrances, life can radiate

All the different chrysalis, life can develop within

I see all the different shapes as love twists

All the different names of agony

All the different lives

Singing the same music of breath

Yet very different notes.

Charisma of creation.

Kismet of creation.

Existence of life in such different homes

When I behold the same movements of ribs

All same but different hued

I see how much diversity lies

In the meaning of pulchritude.

- (Pulchritude)

To enter once again in these typical cycles

To call it a new day is absurd.

To make today a past, we rise again but

To repeat the past, we rise again.

To listen to the same sound

To behold the same things around

To breathe the same air

To the rules of repetition, we constantly adhere.

To stop this now, maybe

To say no now, maybe

To infringe now, maybe

To these typical rules of this typical galaxy

To create a new world

To live a new day

To defy the stupidity my ancestors did

To welcome a new sun,

To make my world more vivid.

To absorb every strength in the air

To make you stand for the concealed you

To create a fresh aura around

To make the air feel new.

To invite the dawn, the winds will blow

To descry how, to the wind, the new buds will bow

To welcome a new me, I'll rise again

To-morrow.

- (To-morrow)

The white clouds beneath my foot.

The black hardness of the ground

Camouflaged by the soft white.

Every time I traipse

My legs drown,

I fall but it doesn't hurt.

The soft snow opens its wide arms to me

Cover me in its coziness

As my bones cascade down to gravity.

The feeling of goosebumps

Emanates from my blood,

When the cold winds

Touch its lips against my dry skin.

I try to grasp the cotton of snow

But the soft diffuses from my palm

To the colossal floor below.

The branches are sown in snow.

The white owls, white pigeons

All abounding the sky.

When the moon comes up

The air echoes with a wolf's howl.

This is the winter,

This is when the sky cascades snow.

When children are merry

Sculpting their buddies:

With the nose of a carrot,

Eyes of black buttons

At the corner of every street.

Who guards the children with his wooden hands.

At the corner of every street

The life of snow, the snowman stands.

Every patch of color then looks so bright

When the land and air is laden

With snow glow white.

- (Snow)

The Star Garden.

'What are stars, mamma?' a child with eyes like a melting butter says. A cat purring on her lap. Both of them gazing into those depths of the night sky only a child or a cat can enter

Amina smiles at her daughter. 'Stars are flowers that bloom only in the sky'

The child turns her gaze to Amina. The words were stumbling on her lips as if she cannot believe herself, 'The sky is a garden?' at last the child says.

Amina nods with a warmth of memories glinting brightly in her amber eyes.

'...so, the stars fall from the sky when the autumn arrives', the child says under her breath as if she is joining the dispersed pieces of the puzzle together.

BOOK FIVE: The Familiar Walls

DESCENSUS IN CUNICULI CAVUM

The descent into the cave of
the rabbit

The Universe's Games.

'Badshah ka wazeer kon?' he called out in his vanity.

I smiled through the corner of my heart. It was a habit of the universe to create his reign over me.

'Jee huzoor' I said almost not wanting to say it. But this was the rule of the game, and girls are not supposed to cheat.[4]

I was just twelve years old back then but somehow the universe made its way of punishing me if I wronged him. Deducting my points from the game if I made a mistake, which was never mine. It prepared me to spent my breaths under his rule, to give up my dreamed victories, to be always blamed, to be at risk.

And now when I am thirty washing his dirty clothes as untold tales and unfinished poetries pile up in my bosom, I still wash his dirty clothes for he doesn't like the idea of wives crossing the success lines created by husbands. He doesn't like the idea of me creating my reign even in just a part of the world. I am in the game

---

[4] A game consisting of four players. The chits aree folded hiding the written title in it. The four titles aree of badshah (king), wazeer (minister), sipahi (soldier), chor (thief). Each player picks up a chit. The king reveals himself calling out to his minister. Badshah ka wazeer kon? (who is the minister of the king?). The minister then answers the king Jee huzoor (yes sir). The king then orders the minister to guess between the soldier and the thief, still camouflaged. If the minister makes a wrong guess, his points are deducted and instead are given to the thief. *Just because a right person could not recognize a wrong, the wrong becomes the right.*

again. He is the badshah[5], the king. Yet I am not treated like a queen for I have always been his wazeer[6].

Sometimes little games unravel the deeper truths of our lives. Sometimes little games are just enough messengers of the universe. And sometimes you have to keep playing these little games for eternity.

---

[5] King (in Urdu)
[6] Minister (in Urdu)

The voice of a wife.

I should obey you

But you should protect me too.

And me, I am made of many dreams

And my voice in me that continuously screams

In my path to stop not

Oh, how could I let the flowers

I have taken care of, rot.

When you protect me,

Protect my mammoth dreams

Protect my trivial wishes

My eternal fantasies.

Each rose in my garth

And even its thorn.

These are the things

That create me.

They say I am partner subordinate

But marriage, no deal it is

We are no partners,

We share the companionship of fate.

No one can be a master

And no one a subordinate.

To your every behest, must I obey

But even if I refuse, forget not

I am not a slave, nor a prey.

Then why around me are cages?

Why am only I accused?

Why am I made to live?

In the reign of everyone in your abode

Why when I speak,

My stories are left untold?

Why is it okay when you pierce me to bleed?

And not okay if just with words

My limits I exceed?

I am my Allah's

More than I am yours.

Wear your crown, sit on your throne

But if you are the king,

A queen will be I.

Don't break my wings,

Your cages won't cease me to fly.

I would chase my dreams and aims

I would reach them under your auspice

I don't live under your rule,

I live under your aegis.

I'll listen to you and obey

But not bow down

For if you sit on a throne

I too will wear a crown.

I'll listen to you but

Respect me, I am as human as you are

Or any male can ever be

Protect every part that creates me.

My wings, my scars, my aims

My dreams, my raptures, my flames.

I have my duties and I have my rights

You can never ask a sun

To shine less bright

You say your orders I can't defy

Then my wings you are at no right to break

You'll have to let me fly.

I am not a slave to rule,

Not a thing to bid.

I am a creature

That can make the world more vivid.

- (Not A Slave)

The voice of a 20-year-old girl.

Close my eyes, still I

Any dreams can't descry

And when I open my eyes

My dreams break like a glass

Then the broken pieces let me bleed

With a rope tied around me,

I am made to follow what society had decreed.

I run after my dreams

But I am just stumbling in the path.

I have been sowing many seeds,

But the growing roots are pulled from the soil

And no fruits I earn

My paths to my aims, my own loved ones will burn.

A young lady I am with a rapture

That will be killed.

They think there is a gap in my existence

Which must be filled

By a man's bond.

Just because I became 20,

My dreams, my aims they stole.

No female was provided to the Earth

To just marry a man.

We have lives too

Independence was nowhere in my existence

In front of my parent's order, I must bow

And then to your man, never utter a no?

Even though they both maybe wrong.

From the moment I was born,

Till the moment death welcomes me

When could I ever be free?

A female was born to be subordinate

Silent sacrifice and murder have always been her fate.

Murder of herself or her zeal

Maybe girls were never born to feel.

But unluckily we do,

And all is collecting inside.

Any longer we wait, we will burst

And quench our own freedom's thirst.

- (The Death of Reveries)

Marks nahi laogy

To kese kamaogy?[7]

The voices circumfused

No air I can breathe free of it

My little shoulders abused

No time I can spend just to sit.

I am just 7 yet

But stories whisper in my ears

How my family's belly

Famished or full

Depends on my A, B or C.

No matter how much I try

These responsibilities are spoken by the people

These, I am not allowed to defy.

I am just 7 yet.

Don't know the price of rice or bread

But still, I am being told

I am on the onus to get my family fed.

---

[7] If you do not get enough marks, how will you earn? (in Urdu)

Daari nahi ugao gy

To mard kese kehlao gy?[8]

I am 18 now

When I stepped out from the doors

Of their rotting persistent words

When I ceased more to be in blue

They found something else to speak

Something new.

I am 18 now.

I look in the mirror

Just clean skin over my chin

Under my nose

No identity of masculinity

On my thick skin grows.

Every night I apply ointments.

Every day I gaze at my reflection

But no hair, no black strand

Calling a no-beard a man

Is what they can't withstand.

And I am 18 now

---

[8] If you do not grow a beard, how will you be called a man? (in Urdu)

Still, they won't call me a man

Not even a boy at times.

I close my room's door every dawn

Not wanting them to see me

Wanting their words to be gone.

Cursing profanities

On my own body and skin.

No sign of being male

Or anything akin.

Am I not a male now?

I want to tell them I am, but how?

For being a man, I need hair on my face

I want to scrape away my clean skin

For with no beard to obscure it, it is such a disgrace.

Job nahi leyga

To larki kon deyga?[9]

I am 27 now.

Much of them I have known

Somehow amidst their walls

---

[9] If you do not get a job, who will give you their daughter? (in Urdu)

I have grown.

From the break of aurora

Till the moon sets down

I venture everywhere

Rummaging for a job in town.

I have run out of luck

As a wanderer here I am stuck.

My bones ache

My eyes call out to close

Under the gaze of the moon.

But before much age passes

I should find a job soon.

Maybe that was real in this world

Real what they had said

I am on the onus to get my family fed.

Or pese nahi laengy

To kya meri kamai khaengy?[10]

Covered in sweat and mud

All-day drenched in master's scold.

____

[10] 'If you do not bring more money, will you eat my earnings?' (in Urdu). A wife's statement to her husband

All-day my shoulders were in pain

Not more able to anymore hold.

The weight placed on it

Without a thought of mercy.

When the moon over the star smiles

I come back to my small abode

Only to find another load

A new wish, a new desire

For a new cloth or a piece of gold.

With such words

That my reasoning goes untold.

And it is better saved in my ribs

Of how I earn

How much I get in return.

I nod again as I always do

For I can't ask my wife

To grant any aid

For if I do, my respect

In her eyes will fade.

I nod as I always do

And give her the little pennies

I have long kept deep in the closet

And I smile at her pout, I am told to

Because that's what gentlemen should do.

When I keep back my wallet

Now so light as air,

I look at my watch collections

Still so empty and bare.

Believe me

It's not about gender sometimes

These towers of bones and blood

They have become blind.

Now that they have lost their visions

If they don't call you a man

Or a lady with ambitions

Is because they can't see that you are

They are blindfolded

They can only see the dark and not the star.

- (Blindfolded)

Born to amble free,

And become the wind

To let you breathe

That flows in subtle harmony

The wind not amends its direction

Under the universe's hegemony

Oh! How had you ever thought,

Thought to order *the wind?*

It was born wild, it runs wild,

Not to be enslaved, can't ever be

Its freedom follows the rule of perpetuity.

But how can you be explained?

You can never get it tamed!

You can never quell the disturbance it can create,

It can turn its form

To the hurricane and the devastating storm

It's because you know not about it;

About the puissance it can imprison,

Oh! How the oldest palm tree falls on its collision

And oh, you know not,

She was born to amble free

And become a wind to let you breathe

The same wind which devastates strongly

The same wind which you can never enslave

The same wind which creates tempest around

But you know not she can never be tamed

Not born to obey and abide

You know not, you've seen its calm state

Have you ever survived a williwaw it can create?

But you think only males can handle the crown?

Oh! She is the same wind in front of which

A powerful tree bowed down.

- (The Wild Wind)

Here in these grasses;

Among some flesh eaters

There live cannibals

Devouring the luscious peace

Of a creature with a womb.

Here in these lands;

The queen of the night

The round body of light

And little fireflies

That twinkle in a grey sea of clouds

All of it, the dark, the black

The moon, the stars

Here in these lands are portents

To cage them up

Cage the creature with a womb.

A creature that seeks freedom

As much as those curtailed of the

Womb and the curves.

Here under these skies;

A shine of her skin

Is considered an invitation to the men

Dress kind is traded for breaths.

Unveiled skin a crime

That must be paid with her life

On a stranger's bed

Covered in her own blood

She is responsible?

Even if on her own blood sea

She had drowned, she did swerve

Even if her bosom was exposed

Did kisses of death she deserve?

Obscuring her skin is indeed

Allah's words.

The defiance is between her God and her.

The defiance is between Him and His worshipper

That is His to decide.

For her, for you, His fire is equally ablaze.

For if He asked her to veil

He asked you to lower your gaze

And believe a believer,

The skies are shaken when His slave cries.

Here trapped in these airs;

Men rule.

Justify their sins

Men rule.

This throne of masculinity will collapse soon

Your throne stands under His reign.

He is merciful a forgiver,

But He will never forgive His slave's pain.

Beware of justification of your wrongs

You are an assassin

Assassin of His created skin.

I, solemnly, spew revulsion

On your worldly thrones

When in the afterlife, hugged by mud

Womb or not, we all will be bones.

- (Here in these...)

I am the daughter of these skies

The sister of these seas.

Listening to the whisper of the waves

Feeling the touch of the breeze

Engulfing the warmth of the day

Swallowing the serene of the nights.

I am the breaths

Of my city of lights.

Grown in the rickshaw rides

The vacations inhaling the smell of tides

The stumbling on the buses

The art on its windows

The conductor speaking out his lungs

The passengers; all emanating languages.

The voice of Karachiites

I am the breaths

Of my city of lights.

It gave me good to feel

It gave me bad to fix

It gave me the beautiful St. Patrick's.

I embrace its agony

I embosom its shine

I will work on the flaws

For this city is mine.

It gave me my first air

My first Azan

It gave me my words

Made me into a girl who writes.

I am the breaths

Of my city of lights.

It gave me the crescent and a star

On the lands of green

Heat and wool

Tan and sweat

Blood and tears

It gave me everything

It is worth all my fights

For I am the breathes

Of my city of lights.

- (Karachi)

I stand on my rooftop

The mammoth light pink sky

Kissing me. The winds

Whispering passing through my hair.

I behold above

The large pine and its ramifying branches

The patches of sky visible

Between the scattering umber woods

Green still hanging.

My honey skin whiter.

The winds were dry

My lips made a rustling sound

When I speak my ballad

To our strongest tree

Our oldest tree

Right there, its heavy branch resting on our roof

I caress it.

And then behold below

The city laden with life

All cuddling and crouching to themselves

Winter has arrived.

The sun sets early

The dark sets in

The moon shines longer

More stars on the sky's skin.

Yet my tree is still green.

It rests beside me, my pal

Its branch coming out to embrace me

I smile

Looking at the light pink sky

Winter will soon go away

It never for long stay

Here in Karachi.

Even though I love winter and oranges

Yet I smirk,

My honey skin will never go utterly white

While I am under the sun that shines bright

And will keep shining over the city of light.

- (Always Green)

'Iron-hard pillows,

On bark of trees

Thorny carpets to walk on

Dark as if blinded

Metallic air to inhale

The cold atop the cliff'

If that together is my home

I shall embosom it all.

No jasmine's fragrance

Or bed soft as sand

The tranquil on an isle

Would ever then

Could ever then

Tantalize me.

As long as I breathe home;

I smell familiarity

The iron-hard pillows will let me dream,

Yet the sand soft beds would make

My nightmares.

Iron hard pillows could festoon my grave.

Above thorns of my carpet;

Are flowers that shall bloom.

The dark is my night sky

Between two stars.

Atop the cliff,

To listen to the music of sea waves below.

Where you see abject misery

There swells a paradise I know

It's to my home, I find my way to go.

- (Way to Home)

Night without Stars

Could you love the night skies without stars? Could you love the petals with their thorns? And the butterflies with their faces? And the dancing peacock with his feet?

Could you love Karachi with all its flaws?

Anyone can fall for perfection. It's the imperfection that makes love.

Loving home is loving the coal and not the diamond. Loving home is loving the broken roads and not festooned corridors. Loving home is traveling the unvisited roads which kiss your broken hearts. Loving home is loving stones and not pillows.

Loving Karachi has just been the same. I do not love the entity of darkness that had intruded the streets of the city of lights, but I'll love Karachi just the same even if it goes out of light. For when the "city of lights" turns into just a name and not an identity, I'll love Karachi enough to light the pages of my poetries turning them into flickering candles. When the ghastly wrath of the dark will come out as nemesis creating a sand storm, I'll love Karachi just enough to turn the sand storm into a sandcastle.

I'll not love the dark; I'll never love the dark that is hungry for the roads of my city. Instead, I'll love Karachi just enough to become a light myself.

When scars fade the beauty away/ only then the truths behind love stay/ for there are million that adore the night/ only a few that loves those skies/ only those that breathe in the midnight's dark/ even when each star dies. ~ Aim-MON

BOOK SIX: Wordless

PRIMUM, NON NOCERE

First, to not harm

Stars of the Lands.

I knew it, the moment I heard it. It started echoing as hungry waves circumfusing me.

The book was in my hand, my fingers grasping tight on to it to cease the intrusion of the shudders as I heard the call coming from our garage. I closed my eyes whispering all the prayers to let it be easy, for it was too late to ask death to go away once it reached the chosen threshold.

My brother ran in bare feet towards the garage. I could not gather the strength needed. It was when I heard his shivering voice I got up.

She was lying on my brother's palm. Her white and black fur was nothing but layers of dust. Her eyes drying as she swerved. My brother was stroking her on the back. I stood there with everything in me shaking as I recite prayers after prayers, which was the only thing I could do. *Pooh* followed me gazing in silence at the dying sister. It took only minutes for the disease to eat her. It was only after minutes every motion ceased and I fell on to my knees. One year with her and she had now dissipated into the abyss I cannot reach. *Chutki,* we used to call her because she was the smallest of all.

I closed my eyes letting my head fall on to her belly. *Only if we had taken her to the vet, only if people had not forced us to maintain distance from a sick cat, only if people respect those calls which held no meanings yet were not meaningless.* But for the ones with the greatness of languages life holds no worth in bodies out of the right words.

Two years later as my nightmares were being embraced by my mind, I felt a hand grabbing my foot. I half jumped seeing my brother standing by my bedside. He gestured me to follow him out of my room and vanished into the darkness beyond the half-opened door. I squinted at my mother who was fast asleep and then at the patch of sky visible from our window. The aurora had kissed the clouds and the stars were nowhere to be seen.

I looked at the direction my brother had ventured into, bracing myself, for it was the time for Autumn's medicine. He was a twin to Olaf, and they were so alike even I could not tell who was who, at times.

I entered into the sunlight of our lounge and found my brother quivering beneath the skin. His voice was gone but his red eyes told me every word that was not dare spoken. I sigh taking my brother in my arms

'Where is he?' I ask

'Lying on the garage floor' my brother said between teary hiccups.

I haven't bid Autumn farewell; I haven't been there with him through this time and I had no energy to see such lively body lay there without even a strand of life.

I looked at the stars gone away from the sky, taking away with them the stars from the lands.

No, Little Autumn

You are not alone

That world is known for its serenity

That world so unknown.

Don't, Little Autumn

Don't be afraid

Arrivals and departures

Is of what life is made.

Love you Little Autumn

And I will always

For in my bosom you lie

While you are so far in the sky.

Sleep well! Little Autumn

Sleep without any fear

When words of euphony

Will be sung to your ears.

Sorry, Little Autumn

I didn't whisper adieu

Farewell little paws, farewell to you.

Sorry Little Autumn

Sorry once again.

I wasn't enough brave

I can't endure to behold you

Resting in your grave.

O Little Autumn, *I miss you*

O Little Autumn, *Thanks to you*

O Little Autumn, Allah Hafiz;

Alwidah[11]

Sleep well, Little Autumn

Sleep well in nature's bosom.

- (O Little Autumn)

---

[11] Farewell (in Urdu language)

Naming themselves as Humans;

How trivial it is.

Nothing more than a mere stain

On the transcendent sheet

Of this impeccable universe.

Lost their aims

Yet clingy only to their name;

Named as human beings,

As Homo sapiens.

These captives of pride;

Captivating the earth,

Thy; a symbol of disgust.

Just how?

How could you devastate the oceanic beauty?

For mere your luxurious survival

And cut down what gives you air to breathe

Dooming the home of your homes to deprival

And how could you hunt down

Every single thing sharing this earth

Have you never known your worth?

The forest stands to exhale the air

The ocean quenches your thirst

And the morning song you hear

Are those tiny birds, singing out their lungs.

And you? What've you ever done?

Cause of extinction; just because you need fun.

And all those species; now mere a mystery,

You killed them less of fear,

More to majestically wear.

But then how can you so proudly

Call your existence as Humans?

When you only know,

How to pull the trigger.

So ironic; the one who was made vulnerable

To feel the most,

Yet the numbest

To the pain of other survivors.

So, here's the truth; we are called humans

Is just a lie of these mortal liars.

No human is defined to be empty;

Empty of humanity.

No human is defined

To kill of its own kind.

Humans were created to think higher;

Lend an aiding hand to even those not so prior.

Humans were made to unite and shield

The constituents of the diverse;

Only then will they deserve,

A small place in this universe.

- (Inhuman Human)

"Oh, two-legged, you don't possess the Earth.

You don't have any throne to sit on

With which you can reign over the Earth.

Your own crown is your prejudice

Nothing here belongs to you

Not me, not the one I kill,

Not the one who kills me.

My flesh fills my killers

And my kill fills me.

We have no wit, you say

But for mere fun, we never kill a prey.

The deer isn't afraid of a lion already sated

But just a vision of you in the woods

Is like death already fated.

You intrude the wild

But you don't spare us

When your streets we intrude.

You may ruin our home

But not bear us under your own roof.

Just a space we need

Where we can breathe

This world was made to be shared

Mercy was blessed to be spared

The world, you don't share

Mercy, you don't spare

You are so full of you

You forget in this world

Lives someone else too.

O human, you and power may have reconciled

O human, but in the course of humanity

You may never outshine the wild."

- (The Call of the Wordless)

Whenever the night haunts me

Whenever I feel so alone,

It is you that I remember

It is you that I recall.

It is your memory that I tether to

To pick me up whenever I fall.

The staring eyes and each long call

We were there together, every day.

I wanted to see you play

I wanted to see you grow

But there is no perpetuity in this world

I never did really know.

Whenever I close my eyes

And fall into the dark abyss of my soul

I feel there you left a void,

I feel there you left a hole

Where your own sound echoes.

But you planted a flower in me

That never stops to bloom

With all the happy moments we spent together

It fills the vacancy of this empty room

It is your souvenir that you planted in me

Like a star in the darkest night sky

Like that twinkle of ecstasy.

Maybe the sun will never bring you to me

Maybe that's how it is supposed to be.

But no matter how much far we are now

You're with me and me with you, somehow.

Olaf, Autumn, Cookie, Cole

And everyone else

You're the 'happily ever after'

In the stories, my heart tells.

- (Happily, Ever After)

Ways to Shine.

'He didn't make noise through all of it. Only as the process ended, a squeak came out of the vet's room.' my brother told me. 'It was a cry that shook the walls, reverberating through my bones and skull, it stiffened me'

I kept listening to my brother staring at Ginger Bun sitting on my lap. He was as tiny as my fist and somehow claims possession to an amount of brevity, not even my imaginations would dare to keep. He has been with me for two months, when he came to me, he was just a week old.

I glanced at her two siblings jumping on the corner of my bed, he was glancing at them too, eyes moving with each motion. Only if he was able to jump around with them. But I knew he will, someday he will jump and play around. I knew he will make his way out of every pain; he will conquer every ache. I knew he will jump across every wall. I knew he was my star on the land. No matter the darkness around stars always find their ways to shine.

BOOK SEVEN: The Black Angel

ET LUX IN TENEBRIS LUCET

And the light shines in the darkness

The Dark behind the Stars

The police sirens occupy the space in the air turning into distant echoes as Ayaan propels himself forward. These noises are as familiar to him as the sound of his own breath. He runs through the small streets of Karachi, his feet turning before he can even recognize the patterns of the roads. Thirty years in this city, his mind remembers every turn, every path, every obscured way which is generally considered abrupt and his legs following the same old pattern.

After minutes of absconding, Ayaan finally reaches the small steel gate of his old abandoned flat. The wrinkled guard squinting at him with the usual suspicion masking his features. Ayaan, ignoring his call, makes way to the apartment hidden in the shadows of the corner. The damp door opens as Ayaan's footsteps approach it.

'What happened?' a woman says standing at the railing of the door. Her kameez is drenched in stains, the color of the fabric worn away with the passage of time. The dark brown skin of her scarred face is camouflaged in the dark of the corner but Ayaan knows the roads of the scars as heartily as he knows the roads of Karachi.

'I got some gold. Go sell it and buy some food' Ayaan says hurrying his way into the small square which he calls home.

'You stole again?' the woman says, a voice of a flower wilting as she speaks, 'How can you feed our children with such money?'

Ayaan sighs stroking the unruly curls of the little girl lying just skins and bones turned in a comma dreaming about luxuries as food. 'Do you think I like robbing people of their labor's fruit, Kiran? I do it because I will not like the sight of my children starving to death, I do it because there is no other way'

Kiran sits close to Ayaan, her gaze on his hands covered with slits in the skin, fresh blood's stain, and dust. She places her crooked fingers on his hand without even a hint of reluctance, without the fear that the hideous bends of her fingers will meet revulsion. 'My treatments absorb all of your pay, no?'

Ayaan smiles at her a smile the crescent passes to the stars, caressing her swollen thumb with his. 'Do you see the sky, Kiran?' he says pointing at the visage of the star covered dark night looking at them through the opened window with broken railings. Kiran follows his gaze.

'We are now traveling in the dark sky but sooner or later we will reach the golden stars', he says

Kiran tilts her head on Ayaan's dust-laden shoulders 'You are not a bad person, Ayaan. You are nothing that they say you are'

'We are made of both the angelic wings and demonic horns. No one is innocent, no one is guilty. We are all night skies; made up of dark and the stars that shine in it'.

Dark.

Why are you so afraid of it?

Dark.

Why do you hide it under the mask?

Dark, accept it, it's yours.

It's your own night that follows your aurora

It's your own night with your caliginous aura.

A field of roses:

You watered with your mistakes

And with defects, you created

A constellation of your scars

If there was no night in you,

How can there be any stars?

Dark, embrace it.

Dark: pure blackness it is

Dark: where the stars find bliss.

The dark in you is your part

So, the light can still shine

And the stars don't depart.

- (Dark)

The darkness throws its veil on me,

The darkness drinks their sight,

The darkness kills the light,

The darkness is my arsenal

Where my secret weapons hide.

Bitten by shadows.

Wrapped up in the hue of anthracite:

The color of the blinds.

As a shadow in the light.

As a universe when the curtains are drawn.

As a veil, a shield;

For darkness is where we hide.

Every color speaks unique soliloquy,

But when augmented

Every color shares the same fate to turn black

Well, of course, except white.

But again, shadows never leave

When intrudes the light.

- (The Remedy of Black)

Will I lose you if I unveil me?

If I tell you who I am;

Will you still heal me?

I come to you as an angel

Still my fingers are clenched in a fist

Even though my demon is asleep

The clear air feels like a mist.

When I am with you, I am not me

It's only a mere facade you see.

If I just come and tell you something

Would you go away?

The sinner that I hide under the mask,

If I take that off,

Would you be feared away?

I love the touch of your skin,

But I am not drenched in such a sin

To make you breathe in a sinner's air.

I don't want to fill your lungs with my sin.

I am so afraid to let you go

I am so afraid to let you in.

- (The Façade of an Angel)

Close your eyes, O angel

Your demons may feast

When behind the curtains

Stay the colors

And arises the beast.

Whenever you, o angel

Close your eyes and see

You too behold within you

Your darkest fantasy.

There is all black

The blackest of black;

As all the earthly colors

Stay stagnant where they belong.

Yours too, O angel

When your eyelids meet

There is nothing but

Vast blackness beneath.

- (O Angel)

When it comes to you

Spread out its arm

Claws your veins.

A bittersweet harm.

The temptations so ghastly

Leaving you helpless

With no other choice than to obey;

No colors then are seen

No colors but the beauty of grey.

The urges fondle and murmur

The secrets of black pleasure.

When it's done

And gone,

And the world comes back to you

With a new idea of right and wrong.

For when the pleasure of sin ends

It feels no good, my friends.

A colossal monarchy of remorse falls

Crushing you beneath its weight.

You eye yourself abhorrent

You endow yourself all hate.

It feels no good, my friends

When your body defies your rules

Bows down to some phantom in you

But not of you

For never can you own such halt

In your peace, and angelism[12]

It is in you, regardless.

The dark demon with horn and red eyes

The dark demon under whose reign

Your rules, your own body defies.

- (Angelism)

----

[12] *Angelism is not a word of dictionary. But I used it regardless breaking the vocabulary rules. I was hoping there could be a better word for the state of a person in which he tries to imitate an angel staying clear from every fault, hating himself for the dark rules he was born with.

Unfortunately, there was no such word. So, I added this word of my own construction in my poem which defines as:

Angelism: (noun)

A state of a human being trying to amend himself into an angel by imitating the purity and complete innocence of an angel and by denying the inevitable existence of dark every human is born with.

When I met him, I didn't know he made me

I didn't know I was made of him too.

He careened towards me

With a gigantic coffer filled with pleasure.

He was too sweet;

Too sweet that he was poison

Too sweet that he became my addiction.

He came back frequently

In days and nights,

Under the blankets, beneath the lights.

Every time I met him, it felt like a jamais vu

Every time the pleasure felt something new.

He made an Arcady out of hell;

I came under his spell

I want to tear him out of my mind.

Serenity comes when we close our eyes

But we are all afraid of getting blind.

Too sweet is poison

And he was it.

He was something in me I despise of me

He was something in me

That couldn't be separated,

With every inch of my soul, he amalgamated.

I want to tear him out

I want to shred my soul.

He is the pleasure when in the fire I burn

He is the pleasure when in ashes I turn

He has been with me since I was born.

I met him to descry my demonic horns

He is the evil in me, I was doomed to meet

He is poison, he is haunting

But he tastes too sweet.

I am scared when I behold him

In my lights, which through

The mirror reflects on my eyes.

I flinch back and close my eyes,

I don't want my fiend to rise.

- (The Black Honey in me)

The charisma of injury

Is that it'll bleed.

Revenge takes less time to born

than injury to get healed.

And no wit in any adolescence

Can conquer the ferocity of rage

And no sympathy and patience

Can then be freed from its cage.

For here comes the air of vengeance;

Don't give and take,

Take and give, by all means.

Take the pain of their given thwack

Take it, but then give it back.

For must they know: the tables have to turn

The candles die that longer burn.

And they are still burning hate

Let's vice versa our fates.

I don't usually be so cold

But if you so insist,

I'll do what I am told.

- (The Air of Revenge)

Lingering arguments amongst them
On relative ferocity of the beasts.

Some say, "The king of the forests, the lion
With bloodthirsty eyes, greets
And your skin with the veins beneath
Together with the taste of blood make his feast."

Others argue, "Haven't you seen the sharpest teeth
Of the merciless sharks beneath
The blue water running so calm?"

Then there are those who fear the snow
Saying, "None can compete with the gray wolves
Smelling the scent of your blood flow.
Can cause your skin to amend to shreds
Scattered over your own blood beds."

Whilst they argue who can destruct the most
I smile through distance knowing the raw truth
It was no ferocious beast or haunting ghost
Through whom mayhem was born the most.

The feeling of loss and grief in this calm universe

The feeling of death before death, one who imparts

Is no one else, but mankind himself-

A beast aiming directly at vulnerable hearts.

- (Ferocity of the Beasts)

I was stumbling in the woods

When I heard a deer cry;

A lion was close to her child

She could do nothing but helplessly try.

It looked as the baby was so fragile

In vain were going, her helpless trial.

I could see the fear in her eyes

And real agony in her cries.

It was for once I thought how mean is the lioness

How hard-hearted, how merciless.

Seeing a mother plead for the life of her baby,

Something perpetual roused in me.

I rushed to set the baby deer free.

The lioness was so afraid of my sight.

She left the baby and ran away in her fright.

For that time, I was filled with dewdrops of pride

I save a mother's child.

As the deer with her child fled away

The lioness looked so grieved at the loss of a prey.

She slowly walked through the grass to a lane

Where I saw what was giving her the pain.

There again, I saw another mother cried

It was the lioness now

Of hunger now was dying her only little child.

Perhaps the other had already died.

The lioness sang a melancholic song

I thought I did right, but I did too wrong.

I wouldn't have helped if I had known before

That the loss here is a little more.

Seeing her only baby die, at that time

I realized *not everything that looks mean*

Is necessarily a crime.

- (Not a Crime)

The First Smell of the Stars.

Kiran lays down on the rocky floor of their small home, her fingers aching at the joint. Ayaan sits beside her, his clothes wet. With a steady breath, he stares back at the night sky. The stars hanging like golden chandeliers in the black sky.

'Have you washed your rickshaw?' Kiran says touching the wet fabric of Ayaan's ragged clothes.

Ayaan nods his eyes like a mirror reflecting the golden lights of the sky. Kiran stares at him like the moon stares at the sea, 'What is the first thing you will do when we reach the stars?'

Ayaan turns his gaze to her smiling his smile which can make Kiran forget about the roads of anthracite. 'I will return all the lights I stole during our dark days to the people to which they actually belong'

Kiran leans and kisses the dusty hands of Ayaan. *Maybe the black they see is just an augmented version of the brightest colors.*

BOOK EIGHT: Frisson and Fate.

ASTRA INCLINANT, SED NON OBLIGANT

The stars incline us, they do
not bind us

The Color of Blood

It came from the stables; it came when I first saw it. And even from the TV screen, it had given me the wounds only I could see. *The color of blood*

The horse in the movie had wounded its eye, I covered my eyes with my fingers; I saw not a thing more, just the sudden gush of blood coming out as torrents from the wound. The ache traversed through the non-existent world to my skin and my eyes, my breaths settled into harmony with the breaths of the wounded horse. For the next few moments, all I could ever hear was the horse neighing in pain, all I could ever feel was the mounting of blood to my eyes, all I could ever see was nothing; for with the horse, I too was going blind.

I did not wait for the movie to end; I ran away crawling into my mother's arm. Every time I closed my eyes, I saw those wounded eyes and the pain came back. It was not fear, though I was afraid. It was not pain. It was as if *the injuries have a telepathic magic*. It was the horse's blood being lost but I, who was going anemic.

And for weeks, the moans and cries of the horse never left my side. The sight was right behind my eyelids. The color of blood and the cries of pain ventured to fabricate the falling towers of my nightmares keeping a five-year-old Aimen awake at nights. And since then the color of blood, the visages of injuries, the slitting of skins and moans from the people in pain made me feel wounded.

Slowly everything in my body urges to avoid such sights and sounds that held the power of rule upon its senses. My body gets so scared that the moment other's pain touches me, I fall into darkness, into the well-filled by their blood and echoing cries. My eyes close themselves the moment blood comes ahead, my ears deafen themselves to let go of those sounds, and my skin numbs itself so that it doesn't feel the hurt coming from their injuries.

I can never explain to the people what phobias are like. I can never define the fear larger than the fear itself. People can never know not every war can be conquered. In the end, the gravity always wins and the rain pours down, stars fall down and my weight melts down.

Only a drop of this color of blood is enough to make whole of me bleed.

Moans and groans

Fabricate a wall around.

The sound stretches its claws

To my bones

And echoes within

My hollow zones.

The shudder reverberates

And my lungs sing out

A lugubrious hymn,

A melancholic rhythm

Emanating into the void of air

Announcing the very secrets of my fear.

My face telling the truth in the fables

Stories of real neighs from the stables

Unknown meanings of the

Language-less words from the cradles.

Just like that my fears are being told.

When the sounds form a wall around

every whisper is echoed.

Sights and sounds sometimes

Are so satirizing

They take no effort to caress

The agonizing.

They take no time to turn into nightmares.

When every sense of you eats your weight

Leaving behind the walls of fear;

So high that even if you want to touch the light beyond,

You would not dare.

You *could* not dare.

For sometimes the fear is larger

than just *a fear*.

- (Phobia)

What shakes you?

Something which I know not

A mystery?

Nay, uncertainty

Of what?

Something without a warning or announcement

To me, will be brought

You fear elements of surprise, why?

Umbrellas are carried only when

Warnings are spoken by the sky.

You fear not being armed?

And not prepared

No one knows the weapon of your past

So, when comes the sudden nemesis

Don't face him aghast.

Fool him that you already are armed

Protected, no longer can be harmed.

How will deception be any wiser?

No one harms a kitten

That wears the skin of a tiger.

- (Future)

The blood churned.

The heart touching the breast bone.

Lungs filling full

Lungs emptying even vacancy

But still, the air got stuck in the throat.

Something got offered the death blow;

Something just cracking its eggshell.

One life killed; one life born

And there the girl stood.

Within her, a grave was dug

Within her, was welcomed something new.

Exhaled at last

All the remnants of that dead

Yet some new breaths swelling her chest.

A sword drowned to her neck

Her reflection glinted

On the blood hued weapon so near.

But alas! The attacker didn't realize

A strength was born when she just killed her fear.

- (The Birth in Funerals)

The Secrets of Fate

Today when I stood in the hospital ward; the horse came back to me only wearing different skin, emanating different pain. And it came from every bed of the alley, it came as blood in drips, as fractured legs, as crying patients. It came from every side ruining me from every angle. My skin then could not go enough numb to erase all the wounds, my eyes could not go enough blind to obscure every sight, my ears could not go enough deaf to let all the cries go unheard.

And now when I say "I don't want to become a doctor" it's not only my love for literature, or my ardor for writing, or my seeking of home, or me avoiding people, it's also the color of blood, the falling of stars, the leaving of the dark. It's the winning of gravity. It's the fate telling the stars they came to a beautiful place they weren't meant to be, for there was another much beautiful place waiting for them.

The horse has been stuck with me and I had always cursed it until I entered the wards where I heard it said, "Every feeling that wraps its arms around you is just fate whispering its secrets."

BOOK NINE: In the Words of a Dreamer.

IN SOMNIS VERITAS

In dreams, there is a truth.

The Night Companion

His unruly curls fall upon his hazel eyes as they grimly gaze over the moonlit visage of the small village. Ismael smiles as he beholds the old baba in ragged clothes walking the side lane carrying a crooked stick in one hand and with the other blankly waving towards the sky. It is the third night he is seeing the same baba waving at the emptiness of the night sky.

'What are you waving at, baba?' Ismael says, his eyes moving towards the sky.

The baba squints at him. A grimace firmly placed upon the folding wrinkles. He nods after a minute of consideration. 'That star…' he says pointing at the sky.

Ismael follows the trail of the old finger up to the thin night clouds. '…but there are so many stars' he says, 'which one are you waving to?'

The baba squints at him as if he is looking at some fool. 'That star…' he says again.

Ismael follows the trail of the finger again yet each time he sees a constellation. 'Why are you waving to a star?' he says.

The baba smiles through the dispersed lips of old age. 'He is the traveler of the skies watching over me. He is beside me through the lonely roads of nights. My friend, he is following me all around. How could one not wave to his friend, one can neither touch nor have the taste of'

'Your friend?' Ismael says glancing up beyond the clouds

'You have one too, kid. The night sky gifts one star to each person beneath its eye' baba says limping his way and waving at that one star only baba knows.

At this moment under the ticking of a distant cricket and showered by the light of the Lady Moon, Ismael turns his face up towards the sky, ambling through the stoned roads of his small village. And there he finds it. He finds her. That star. A star tethers to his heart following every path Ismael takes. At this moment the sky turns into a home and stars turn into millions of dreams of millions of people turn into a companion of night.

I am the traveler of these roads

With dark above me, and gray below.

Beholding the moonlit visage of Karachi's streets

A star tethers to me, follows where ever I go.

In the emptiness of night roads,

My feet's tintinnabulation echoes

But the sky gives me a star

Wherever I go, it goes.

Although it is with me, close abroad

But I can't catch it,

My fingers can't reach it.

If just there were stairs to the sky

I would have caught it, kept it

My hallowed sparkle

So that it won't vanish away with the sun

If just I caught the star that follows me

I could have filled the void of darkness

That hollows me.

I am the wanderer of this soul

With nothing above me, nothing beneath

Beholding the depth of this charismatic abyss

A dream tethers to me, be where ever I am

In the nothingness of this soul

My heart's whispering beats echo,

It has provided me with a dream

Which goes where ever I go.

Although it is in me, so within the reach

But I can't catch it

My fingers won't reach it.

If just there was a path down this abyss

To its greatest depth, my chest;

I could have walked to my bosom

Where my little dreams rest.

If just I reached my dream that follows me

I could have filled the void of nothingness

That hollows me.

- (If Just)

Store it in humps of your heart

Like a camel wandering on sands

To quench his thirst and

Feed himself when famished;

For the grains

Won't fall in rains,

The clouds don't will to emanate

You have to carry your own jewels

To adorn your own fate.

Store your beauty in your bones

In your blood.

In the form of glyphs, they don't understand

For nothing can savor

What's stored in the camels of the sand.

Touch the taste of manumission

Through the rough deserts of life.

The water in blood is mixed

The nourishment on your bones is carved;

So, while ambling through the desert of life

You don't fall starved.

- (Camels of Sands)

As the wind flows

And collects every exhale

It abounds with all that people emit

Then I inhale, I take all of it

Inside my throat and into my veins.

The exhales of the people

With doubt's scars and abasing stains

I breathe in.

Breathing is from where our lives start

But breathing pulls the same toxic wind

Into my throat, veins and to my heart.

The poison in the air scrapes away my dreams

Can people heal it?

When they pollute the air.

I inhale what you exhale

Our exhales are what make the air

Don't flood it with your doubts,

Criticism and fear.

For all those things which come

Along with the air

It molds everything inside;

It kills the waves and silent the tides

But what do I do?

To live in this world, I need to

Breathe.

'Breathe not', everything inside me screams

But to live I ought to breathe

So, I'll live by the memories of my dreams.

And by these twinkling glimpses of memories

I'll run, breathe hard, and run so far

For my soul isn't curtailed of dreams

Even when realities are.

- (Exhales)

The ticks of the clock;

Hands moving away,

That hour moving closer:

The hour of my war.

In a battlefield then

I'd have to stand

No mercy spares the clock's hand.

Trepidation swallows me

My courage nowhere to be seen.

I am shivered by the thought of

Mere confrontation;

Let alone conquering.

All my wisdom, all my grit

All my strength, all my wit

Vaporing away.

The hour of battle is near

Pulling closer the fear.

I closed my eyes.

I can either fight

Or enjoy the night.

Either way,

My risk of death hangs thick in the air;

Either way, I cannot ignore the fear.

Fighting it will give a strand of hope

To celebrate my triumph.

I stand.

I walk.

All armed.

In the field now.

The hour is there.

There is a risk of dying

and

A hope of victory's air.

So, I fight now

To kill all my regrets.

Fight now.

For the hope.

Either way, there is a colossal risk

Of me dying.

So even if my fate bears death

Why don't die trying?

- (Death in Attempt)

The absurd ardor canst make thou amble

Even if what thou lack is a pair of legs.

The fervor in thy heart makes it beat.

The thirst of thy lungs; the reason thou breathe.

Through ages this zeal

Had evolved resistant to evanescence

Adamantine to ever fade

Regardless of unannounced ambuscade

Sewn by people's tongues.

But not thou know;

What shall be carried by thee?

To shield the path to thy ecstasy?

Faith, folks

Faith is all, folks;

Faith is the bowl empty

Only to create enough vacancy

For thy vehemence to rest in.

In the darkness of mediocre,

Illuminate thou with faith's glow

So that thou could be endowed with vision

A path to aim is all it could show.

Faith, folks

Thy faith in thee.

No matter the ambush predators

If thou need aught

It would be

Thy faith in thee.

Regardless of the people's push

To make thou fall down

Faith, folks

For the way is already found.

Maybe it is not under the light now

But one day the way thou canst see

Have this much of *thy faith in thee.*

- (The Absurd Ardor)

It's okay if you can't reach your dreams

It's okay if you failed then, and you failed now

Take relief,

You are not falling into abeyance;

Every event makes you who you are now.

Every step you take

It's your story they endow.

So, what if you are falling

Keep the fire ablaze

You can't be disused

The dreams were meant to make you chase.

Even if the lion fails to capture its prey

He will still wear the crown

Still a monarch he will stay.

It is because he chases

The deer are afraid

It is because he chases

There is rapture in his gown

It is because he chases

He still wears the crown.

And maybe while you chased your chimeras

You got the blood that flew,

You held the wind that blew

You got mounted up as a mammoth you.

Maybe no one told you,

But I shall surely do:

'Every dream must be chased

But not each can be held in hand;

This chase leads you through stairs

Crawling through which, one day you will stand.'

Not every ice turns to water

Not every water flows

Not everything has a core

Not every dream can be caught

But every chase gives you so much more.

Failure is success in its own way

Not a thing you and I should abhor.

- (The Chase)

She is there, under the water

She is there.

The turtle seeing the visage of unseen

Wandering through the waves of the sea.

The call came; unexpected.

Something so protected,

So, sacred in her womb

Wanted to come out, must come out.

An uninvited call from nature.

By the voices mounting up to her brim

The turtle, nonetheless, started to swim,

To the shore, she has to make

To give the lands what was within her:

A promise she once did undertake

To the shore, she began

Moved her fins,

Moved ahead, as fast as she could

Towards the north, towards the sand.

Sometimes it felt as if her energy

Not even the waves could withstand;

For the water flew

But then it stopped.

Water flew and pushed her ahead

But when it stopped

It was hard to find the way

When the water stopped, it was hard to search

As if on a mammoth floor,

She had lost a thread.

The pause in waves, but no pause in fins

She swam and, slowly but, still moved ahead

On that giant floor, there was surely the thread.

The water stopped and it flew

She never paused

And made it through.

And when her legs touched the sand

The sacred entities within her

Came out to bless the land.

The water flew, but it stopped too

Still, she made it only because,

The pause of the waves never made her pause

- (She Never Paused)

You are the sun;

Setting down to rise high.

But once you are up,

You dazzle the sky.

See, no one can jump higher,

Without touching the ground.

It's only when the lights are off,

The moonflower blooms around.

The energy in its prey

Keeps the hawk flying with its crown

And even the hawk for its quarry,

Needs to come down.

See, only the one who keeps walking

Are vulnerable to fall.

How could you not get hurt,

While breaking the walls?

See, every bird falls,

Before it gets to fly.

You are that bird;

Falling before you touch the sky.

See, if you're willing to walk,

You will fall.

Because those who don't,

Are the ones who just sit.

Failure is not an antonym of success;

Failure is the road to it

- (The Failing Success)

Once inked down in the pages of past

The words forever last.

Every success, every fault of you

No denials can erase it

For the words of *the book of time* are true.

If your arrow had fallen,

And not hit the mark

Time had captured it.

Never can you erase the ink's stain

That speaks out, 'there was a fall'

It is extant in those rust of pages

So, when you visit the book of memories

You can truly recall

Your arrow had a fall.

Not born you were a prodigy or portent;

There was a tedious journey

A monotonous succession of pages

An avalanche of your stories of the fiasco

Of arrivals and persistence of your nemesis

Of the roads, how you reached your arcade

Your bliss.

Such that as one by one

The pages will be turned

You will know, you weren't born good

It was a process of how you learned.

It will make you able

To accept failures and failing

It will make you know your ailments

And make you do the ailing.

Page by page, word by word, ink by ink

Your petals will glow.

Page by page, word by word, ink by ink

Your branches will grow.

And even if you had been trying hard

And rendezvous with only falls, only downs

Go on with your life, not fault yours

Your mistakes, do not overthink.

For if you have the pen of your time

It is your luck that has the ink.

- (The Time's Book)

"Shape me", she said as I stood staring at her image

Reflecting from her eyes was that passionate rage

"Shape me", she said again, "my mind, my body.

Make me the version you'd love to be."

I nodded, I knew she was meant to

And for her, only I have the pen to adorn.

But then they threw a stone,

The mirror broke; she was gone.

"Shape me", it said as I stood against the lights

"Shape me like the visions you see,

When you close your eyes."

I nod, I knew it was meant to

And the visions were within only my eyes

But then they closed the lights;

The black silhouette was engulfed by the dark around

But I know the visions, in my mind, are still profound

Profound and alive

I nodded, I knew only I can make them survive.

I ran outside to the sunlight

In my Nike shoes and dumbbell in my hand

It was there lying on the ground with a dumbbell too

I smiled at it saying, "I shaped you.

They turned off the lights but they can't stop the sun

I shaped you like my visions, your muscles burn."

I ran again now with brushes and pens,

And a stack of classical romance in my hands

She was there again on the calm water of the ocean

Grasping tight onto the novels, brushes, and pens

I smiled at her saying, "I shaped you.

They can break a mirror, not the ocean

You can write it down, write all the emotions

And paint the pictures with all your devotion."

So that's what I did, I fought to earn

I shaped my shadow in the sun,

And reflection in the ocean

I shaped my mind, my soul, my body

I created a version of myself I love to be.

- (The Version of Me)

The clouds of aurora ambling

Over the eastern line

Where the sierra abuts the sea.

The velvet before my window

Is drawn away.

Staring at the golden waves of the sea

My eyes still behold thee.

The rise of the dawn ahead;

But I am no more able to sleep.

Thou canst come to my hands

My fingers canst touch thee

But people's words nestle

Amidst thou and me.

A call from an expergefactor[13]

O my! I need not

My aurora adorns with naught

But the thick thought;

Wide awake it keeps me.

Wherefore dost thou not reach me?

Thou art naught

---

[13] Alarm or anything that wakes you up.

Yet

Thou art my air.

Not seen by the eyes around

But me? I can fill my bosom

With thy sound.

Dost thou, o, come to me.

Thou art my dreams

My will-o'-the-wisp is thee.

Canst I catch thou?

O, I nod my head.

Kiss thou, embosom thou

And be festooned by thee.

I am thee, thou art me.

My dream, my aim

My air, my name

Thou art everything

My words, my poetry

Thou keep my eyes wide open

Thou I see when I close them.

Thou art the vision

Thou art the emotions

I behold

Thou art the reason

For which a pen I canst hold.

- (Thou Art Everything)

Why the clock is so small?

Why the second's hand moves so fast?

As if it had stolen the speed from the air

Its speed my little hands cannot bear.

For they get tired and pause

But the clock? Why doesn't it cease?

Traveling for time is a breeze.

Nights come, day goes

While the chirping of dawn birds still echoes.

Why only twenty-four?

Why not more?

Why every day is of such a miniature size?

I flap my wings and the day vanishes away

I can never make it to the skies.

Why is it too small to fit my dreams?

Why are my dreams too large to fit in?

I don't have control over either.

My hands are tied with ropes of the dilemma;

I want to move but I couldn't.

So less is the time

So small is the clock

So quick is its hand

So large is my dream

Not the speed of time can be abated

Not my dreams I want to belittle.

The runners of time run ahead of me

But I just do what I can do

I keep crawling

What if late, I shall still make it through.

- (The Speed of Time)

Chasing Stars.

Was it him chasing the star or the star chasing him?

Ismael ran through the night streets, the star running with him. Stopping when he stopped. He missed the baba now for there were millions of question tipping on his tongue. The only one he remembered at times like these was *"are there ways to catch the stars?"*

He stood panting, looking at the stars that were talking to him through the silence of the night. 'Did you come to give me a taste of the chase?' Ismael said to the blinking golden star looking back at him.

The star blinked.

'Are there ways to catch you?'

The star blinked.

Ismael smiled looking beyond the golden shine to the uniform of a pilot on his shoulders. He smiled looking at the star itself. 'I have ways to come to the sky to catch you', Ismael grinned.

The tiresome days and haunting nights, the fear given by people and graves of hopes dug, the lonely roads and strange homes; nothing mattered but the star. Nothing bothered him but the uniform of a pilot as a cape on him. It was magic to Ismael himself. The chase and its perpetuity. The chase and his will to run after. It was a miracle to him itself.

Is it the dreamer chasing the dream or the dream chasing the dreamer?

BOOK TEN: Death and Life

MEMENTO VIVERE

Remember to live

MEMENTO MORI

Remember that [you will]
die

Fire in Night Sky's Ocean.

Izaan looks at the grey stone reflecting the golden light of the sun. Repeating the name carved on it as soft whispers to himself. He stands at a little distance from the mourning crowd.

A bearded man limps his way beside Izaan, the wrinkles on his skin emanating histories.

'Muazzam was the only shoulder to his old mother' the man says with a voice like a museum flooding with forgotten fables of the past.

Izaan glances at the old bearded man failing to recognize him, 'who are you, baba?'

The man shakes his head, 'Like Muazzam, my son too forgot the truth that even killers can be killed.'

Izaan traces the trail of the man's glance resting on the grave neighboring to Muazzam and suddenly feeling a rush of sympathy. 'You are Muazzam's colleague's father?'

The man nods. 'He was my only shoulder, my shield' the man sighs a sigh which tells stories of sorrows without a word being used. 'Who knew time will attack the protector and not the protected.'

Izaan glances at the clouds above him and the hidden stars in the sky of the sun 'The stars, you see, have beautiful lives yet the chosen ones only die to shine in night skies. They were both soldiers like fires fighting ice. And in trying to melt the ice, the fire always seems to forget the water'

You may breathe the air

That for me must be a venom

You may memorize the glyphs

I cannot bear to fathom

You can mourn over a tragedy

And I may be numb.

You can let go of a loss

I can't help react to it

You can wear a cape

That on my shoulders doesn't fit.

You can speak the words aloud

That I may only murmur

The same rope tangles around my neck

That you hold on to as a tether

The same load can be heavy iron for me

Which for you is a mere feather.

But maybe I embrace those visions

Which for you are phantoms

I embosom the fire

Which melts you down

Maybe silk cascades down my neck

And you can't handle a gown

Maybe my strength is your weakness

And your power my fears.

Even If I am the fire;

You may be the ice

I can be extinguished

You can melt away.

We both are mortal;

Weak we are

But reaching our culminations

Brutal we are.

With the finesse to kill others

And each other.

But still, you will melt away

Into liquid crystal clear

And I can flicker to death

By the touch of air.

- (Mortal Killers)

So very calm is the air

The restlessness lies in me;

No one here is a victim of time

But time attacks suddenly.

Here comes a moment of epiphany

When the thought so paralyzing

Suddenly strikes me.

My beloved connections and even me

All vulnerable to time

I cannot bear this vulnerability

For every moment passes in fear

What if the next one brings the attack near?

Will I be able to spread my wings?

Around every person I love

And my sacred hallowed things.

Will I be able to be their escutcheon?

Can I hold them under the aegis of me?

What if I am attacked instead?

I would likely die; I will not bear to surrender.

Can I persist to be their defender?

When time is such a universal killer.

It brings death before death arrives

It kills hope, no dream survives.

Even if my wings cover the entirety;

I am afraid this shield is too weak

For it cannot itself strive

When attackers of time arrive.

How will I be able to defend all of you?

What can I and what should I do?

I pledge my troth, solemn am I.

I will not end to surrender

I'll stop when I die.

But survives a void, in my defense

This void I know not can be filled

For how can I stand to defend you?

When time will get me killed?

- (The Death of Shield)

Should I feel gratitude?

To be brought in this universe

When I can't understand

Is this a blessing or a mere curse?

The wings of cages surround me;

And there is no air to breathe

I am not running but my legs are tired

I want to reach a destination;

But I roam as a wanderer

I want to climb the stairs;

But now my legs are paralyzed

I want to breathe fresh air;

But in a cage, I am ghettoized.

To survive is not an easy task to do

You live when you start being you

But a mask is worn by I, you, we

So even when I exist in this universe

There is no me.

To breathe here is a sacrifice

Why do we mourn when we demise?

When funerals should be the thing to celebrate

From then on, the dead has only peace in his fate

No more suffocation

No more heat

No more wanting of air

No more agony

No more caging fear

To born was a curse

Trying to fit in this universe

Is even worse.

This place shatters every dream

Mammoth is this place;

It turns to whisper, even when you scream.

We are born, just to one day die

We fear falling but want to reach so high.

Living is a curse because it gives you pain

Living is a curse; you'll lose everything you gain

Living is a curse, not because it will end

It's a curse because we don't know when.

Maybe today we worked, and tomorrow we die

Maybe we had placed the stairs

But could never touch the sky

- (The Curse in Life)

Not everything can be a fantasy,

I have to wake up from my dreams,

Not every dream can be ecstasy

I have my nightmares, my screams.

I may escape reality

But it comes and hits me back

And leave me on my knees

Where I open my arms to death.

Inhuman, as it is

It never comes when called.

The misery spread through my chest's breadth

Life is infamously called stern

When so is death.

I yearn for it; I call for it

But

No death will arrive, while I need;

No one will take the life out of me

To render my spirits healed.

- (The Ailment in Death)

Every night comes out the same moon

But each night is beautiful.

Every day the same sun rises in the Eastern sky

Radiating light for everyone to descry.

Every day the angels pray and the sinners sin;

Every day is same but every day is different.

Some moments in a garden,

You'll breathe in the fragrance of a rose

But there will be time

You'll inhale the burdening black air.

Forget not, life never gives you burden

Your shoulders can not bear.

Every day someone may die

But everyday light pierces through the sky.

Every day a chrysalis breaks

When a caterpillar turns into a butterfly.

Pain is inevitable

Inexorable it is

Misery and bliss,

Life it is.

Every day the sun rises

Every day the lands invite you.

Every day won't be the same, every day won't be new

The same things change every day

And one of them is you.

Life is a pain but it is worth living

There will be dark around

But there are colors we keep seeing

- (The Different Beauty)

When you climb stairs,

There is always a risk to fall

When you swim,

There is a risk to drown.

When you fight,

There is always a risk to bleed.

But with each risk you take,

The beast in you, you feed.

Take risks, some pain you can bear

To overcome it, we were all given fear.

When you hide, you are afraid of being caught

So, stand on the battlefield, and be afraid not.

Cause each time you stand to take risks

It weakens your weaknesses.

Fear was given to be fought;

Pain was given to be endured.

We hide just to be caught

So, break your cages, come out

And be afraid not.

See, death comes when it comes

It's a rule you cannot defy

So, don't you stop living

Just because you're too afraid to die.

Climb the Everest,

Stand on its edge and below you descry

You can come back or fall off and die

But you'll die a person

Who got his dreams fulfilled

And not someone who was hiding

But eventually was killed.

Take risks you'd love to take

Break the cages, you'd love to break.

Till when will you keep hiding

From the things that fright you?

So, what if you didn't die today?

You'll always be the prey.

And death is such a deadly predator

It always finds its way.

Take risks, come out, and endure some pain.

Don't live under fear's rule

You have to create your own reign.

- (Risks)

When the world goes dead

And the soil all barren.

The roots all dry

And the leaves all fallen

When the breeze goes stale

And petals wilt down

When blood leaves a trail

And green ambles into brown

When the water is all steam

Yet the sun is just a mere gleam

When the words you write

Construct nothing but an obituary

When stones of grave replace pages

And soft mud forms the cages

Nature will melt around you

And you will be frozen

A heavy adieu;

A sacrifice for the chosen.

- (Death)

Dead Stars

At night Izaan sits on his favorite spot at the *dhaaba* he and Muazzam used to visit on the nights of Saturdays. He stares at the lonely cup filled with hot tea, smoke churning up towards the sky forming clouds

'Muazzam was a man of great honor', the baba of the dhaaba says finding his place beside Izaan.

Izaan nods in the blank space of air.

'It is devastating to hear our youths dying' baba says

Izaan glares at the dead stars on the sky still shining like fireflies, 'Shaheed never die'.

Baba pats him on the back just the way he always used to.

It is the first time Izaan is haing a Saturday night.

BOOK ELEVEN: The Wings of the Pages

CALAMUS GLADIO FORTIOR

The pen is mightier than the sword

Meanings of the Mountains

It's when the eyes of an artist open, the curtains fall off and the secret behind unravels itself. It's when the heart of an artist burns, the world turns into home. And it's when the pen of an artist gets a paper, the colors begin to flow.

The mountains arc around the narrow road as a semicircle stretching beyond what the eyes can behold, yet not beyond what the art can peruse. As I gaze the mountains, the crisp wind flowing by my hair through the gaps of my hijab, a question breathes in me. Like every question, this too is the very child of the artist in me. *What makes the mountains stand?*

Maybe it's the hopes of the scattered sands to dwell together. Maybe it's magic of the roots of the tiny trees growing in the mountains. Maybe it's the prayer of the homes standing atop the mountains. Maybe it's a spell the clouds have cast. Or maybe it is an art that makes the mountain stand. A mere art of piling up flowing sands. A mere art of creating.

And maybe for you, it is just sands tied together. Maybe for you, it is the children's wishes or where the dead bodies get lost. Maybe for you, the mountains have different meanings.

Maybe mountains *have* different meanings for mountains are art.

What are the mountains for you?

Meanings are born;

Meanings die

Every time the words welcome

a new eye.

The silken thread of black ink

Woven over the pages

Festooning some zeal.

And somehow yet not breathing

They know how to heal.

And once you turn over the page

The stories won't end;

It will begin

With a new meaning.

For every glyph is born

With unvisited possibilities,

With a constellation of galaxies.

You were invited to mere one of all

The one which could hold only you

Whenever you stumble to fall;

The world with your little naïve footsteps

Marking its sand.

The threshold you crossed

The moment the page was touched by your hand

Or maybe your eye.

Maybe new meanings are born

But the old ones never die;

They dwell and abide

Within the abode of pulsing hearts.

And this is how with every reader

In the same old words

A new story starts.

And I hope the world which you enter

When you have closed the book

Lives in your heart, ambles in your blood.

And it is no myth, my friends

That a single stroke of the pen

Has so much magic to give

To the ones, who within the words

Create their homes and live.

- (When Words Turn into Home)

A strength, a finesse

A magic I can see

Which no eraser can eliminate,

No color can camouflage.

Sometimes my *teer*[14];

Sometimes my *taaj*[15].

A gold crown of hubris;

An arrow that never misses its aim.

Breaths breathing abreast me.

The pen; the words; the worlds

Everything I have; everything I can be.

(Everything I Have)

---

[14] Arrow (in Urdu)
[15] Crown (in Urdu)

I feel like deserted isles

At the dark corners of the ocean

Left alone with soils barren

And winds utterly dry.

Winds blow there as storms

From all the sides of the world

From up, down. Left and right.

Where there is no warmth of the day

And no beauty of the night.

I feel the slits of my skin

Deepening into an abyss of blood.

I am dying with thirst

Yet drowning in flood.

Every thought crashes on me like iron chains;

There is so much of it

That I could not name the pains.

Like there is a storm around

Yet you can't get the taste of air.

Should I tolerate?

Should I give in?

And endure all that agony

Not worth my endurance?

No, readers, I am not the kind

To suffer what should not be.

So, I take my ailment

Hold my pen

And sit while dying

To be what I am.

My pen loiters on the pages

Just to define the cages

And the feelings trapped in my bones

And the rushing of blood

And the thirst of lungs.

I write down death while dying

Ink down the emotion of loss

While a bloody war I fight

For there is no feeling that could go waste.

No feeling a pen cannot write.

- (Deserted Isle)

My words were like a blurred picture of pain;

You could not comprehend it

But you realized how haunting it would be

Being secreted from the broken parts in me.

My verses reminded you

About the existence of agony.

And my poetries were a Kalashnikov

Loaded with graves of my tranquility

Aimed to create mayhem in your heart.

It is because my tongue was manacled

my pen's rescue had to start.

Though I design my words dangerously

They are still just water drops

Of my silence- *the scariest sea.*

I know yet my silence is not heard

because I befriended with each word.

The greatest combination for the scariest fighter

Is a pen with a paper in the hands of a writer.

- (I am a Writer)

Drink the beauty of dandelion

In your wine,

Smoke the fumes of creation

In your cigar;

Then do it, in intoxication

Do it, in oblivion

O artisan.

Just do it when your heart is unafraid,

And your mind carries no thought,

And your tongue emits all that it must.

Do it when the lectures of politeness

And manners you bunk.

Do it, O artisan, only when you are drunk;

Drunk with the beauty of dandelion

When fumes of creation fill your lungs.

And if you feel empty of it;

You feel void

Stroll down to your core

Where there is the finest alcohol,

The ancient cigar,

And the rarest wine.

Drink it through your veins,

Inhale it in your blood.

Get addicted, O artisan,

To the smell of the heavenly smoke,

To the taste of that empyrean drink.

Make not, create

Under the realm of the wine

As *'To make is human,*

To create is divine'.

- (O Artisan)

I don't have words now to give

O paper, O pen

Still, I'll hold you, O pen, and make you my sword;

I'll collect you, O paper, and make you my wings.

O paper, O pen

My sword, my wings

My possession, my way to my heaven

In this fight, or in any phase of my breaths

I am not alone, *never alone*

I can touch my paper, hear my pen

Even in this hell, I can escape to my heaven.

O paper, O pen. You are of my blood

- (O Paper, O Pen)

Not traveling to different countries or towns;

I've wandered through so many worlds.

Each night when all the eyelids meet,

Mine stay apart to taste how it feels,

How it feels to stay stagnant and still

Yet traveling under the magic of a quill.

Each night when all the eyelids meet,

Mine stay apart because my mind insists

Traveling is something my body can't resist.

My eyes travel down every line within the pages;

While my soul travels to places that don't exist,

When every eyelid around the world is closed;

Mine stay apart because they have idyll, diagnosed

- (Traveling)

Not down long ago

There were entities

That crumpled, made sounds

Like the waves of different seas;

All deep, all ecstasies.

Like the ebony escape gate

Hidden in deep shadows;

All colors like the deepest greys

Camouflaged by the vapors of haze.

The colors lie in oblivion.

Though the haze made my eyes blind

But my visions were the moon-smellers

Gazing something, they could not find.

The anthracite melted as a rainbow in me;

Like falling from the stars

Are the colors of the sea,

And the lilac of the sky,

The amethyst of the desires.

Trapped in the iris,

All the ceruleans and sapphires.

Some shades disembogue

From the emerald sierra.

All the shades of the horizon, I behold

While the walls around me;

 Stories of black they told.

The colors I could see

Came out as torrents from me

From within the gaps of my every rib;

Decanting into my pen's nib

Curling into strands of ink

Forming glyphs and words

From which the black can drink.

I wrote colors on the black

Loving the words that

Loved me back

- (Black Can Drink)

My eyes, words they drink

Words that smell like a flower

Made of ink.

And just as I drink them

I am under a spell;

These motifs on pages

Become roads and paths

Leading to destinations

With magic and smiles.

While the page is in my hand

It lets me taste coffees, ciders, and teas

Lets me know magic and tragedies

Feelings I have never felt

Visions I have never seen

Voices I have never heard

Places I have never been.

All these in the roads

of the curves and shapes

Of every alphabet

Every word.

Doesn't it seem a miracle, o reader?

A spark of magical shimmer and shine;

That some little book

Can hold in itself an entire universe,

And that some beautiful words

Can become roads on which

You can walk with your eyes.

An escape route for you and me.

When the world around you

Collapses down

And you have nowhere to go

You knock at the little magic

And off to the lands of fantasies;

So enchantingly confined within a book.

You escape the ruthless world again

Just opening the pages was all it took.

- (It's all it took)

Stories are foretold, folks

We carry it as crowns on our heads.

The words are recited from birth

Ending on our death beds.

The murmurs of the heart

The passage of air

Tells the fables of survival.

The scars and stains

Unraveling the histories of fights.

The dark under the eyes

Revealing the secrets of the nights.

The hue of the skin

Speaking the labor of the days.

The smile on the face

Announcing the exactness of gaze.

Stories are already written, folks

We just carry them

On our heads, like crowns, stories we hold;

And our bodies with beauty

Every tale, they unfold.

- (Tales)

Calling me *Aim-MON*, I cast on me a spell

Because I *Aim to be the Magic of Nouvelle*[16].

The walls are so high around

But I'll keep writing

Till they are broken down

By the echo of my pen's sound.

I am at still no height

I am still an ordinary,

Anonymous to many.

I have hideous scars, but they prove my fights

And sunken eyes, evident of my work at nights.

I may look sick, but I feel contrary

You mock it, but I value darkness

If there was no dark in the night,

Would the day ever feel bright?

My angels and demons and *mon la bête*[17]

All in me are out of their leash

- (Aim-MON)

---

[16] Novel (In French)
[17] My beasts (In French)

The night falls again.

And I get surrounded

By the mystique of pen,

And create a cacography;

Which then, I bedizen.

I commit to paper,

And give a physical existence

To all that which confine within me

Every fiction, every fantasy,

Every real thing,

Which never can be a reality.

Stories only I can tell,

Words only I can say,

In a way;

Someone else never may.

And yet sometimes,

I create which that no one but me,

No one but me can decipher;

This is the charisma of being a writer.

- (The Mystique of Pen)

Come to me, O ink-bleeder!

Come to give a taste

To those thousand readers.

Make your words float on their chest

Like sea waves on the sand

Soak them in your words

With the spells of your hand.

Chase me, I am the chimera

Only you can hold.

O ink-bleeder, emit your words

The readers need to be told.

Support them, elevate them;

The pages wet by your blood

Would be their scaffold.

Chase me, come to me

For it is you who I am calling.

O ink-bleeder, my call must you hear

For you are the only soul

To which for eternity, I adhere.

Remember the discourse

We had when we made vows;

Before any of us landed on the lands

Before any of us tasted the seas,

Smelled the sands.

O just recall the discourse

"I'll hover parallel to your hub,

Only your core", my oath all solemn;

But do recall your vow

Whenever I'll call you,

Come to me, only me shall you endow.

O ink-bleeder, never do forget

The words of your oath.

Feed the paper, I'll be nourished

The onus is on you

To get your reader's core replenished.

- (Call of Aim)

When words just fill up to my brim

But they resist to be spilled out;

I know I am suffocating

When my body will no longer

Give my words to the pages;

It confines the remedy in my bosom.

I know that I am struggling, when

I so much need my remedy

That I can't share it with my pen.

- (Inert)

If I leave the world,

With my words not finished.

Can you carry my pen?

Will my asset be dear to you?

Can you finish,

What I couldn't do?

So, if I die,

All my poetries

All the synopsis

All my words and drafts

They are treasured in my pages

I have written everything there,

My Arcady, My Eden

I will leave it all here.

I owe them the fealty to get them done

By anyone…

Anyone worthy to hold my asset,

Anyone worthy to share the diamonds mine,

Anyone ardent to make them shine.

I beseech my readers and listeners

If I die

Before getting them finished

Please get them done

In the words of extinct Aim-MON

- (Extinct Aim-MON)

Words in the Night Skies.

The cries circumfused around Akbar as he strolled through the beds of the patients. Some cries were loud enough and some were audible through the silence they carry. He kept following the doctor, the anxiety growing up in him. Where was the doctor taking him? Was something wrong with him? But he was too shy to speak up. Silently, the nineteen-year-old boy followed the doctor. His legs aching from the long bed rest. He kept searching for his mother around the small, smelly corridors of the hospital as they walked. But she was gone to buy Akbar's medicine.

The door opened. The room here smelled less than the actual ward. There were two rows of people; girls and boys of almost his age, wearing white gowns over their shoulders. All eyes were on him as he made his way from between them to the bed. All eyes. He had never been under all eyes. A shudder reverberates through his bones. Quietly, he sat down on the patient's bed. His eyes on the floor.

'Quiet, students' the doctor said. The waves of murmur silented across the crowd.

'Watch and learn' he said as he approached Akbar with a stern eye turned towards his 'students' sitting in white gowns.

'Salam, Akbar. I am your doctor and I will be inspecting your chest and back. Can you take your shirt off?' the doctor said.

Akbar looked at the girls and boys sitting on chairs before him. Their eyes on him. 'Shirt off?' he said under his breath.

'Yes,' the doctor said.

He paused every other moment. But there was no way out. His hands quivered as he pulled his shirt revealing the scarred skin he so preciously had kept under the rose. He gazed down at his bare chest. His fist clenched as embarrassment flushed across his body. *He was wearing a diaper and they were seeing it.*

The doctor started speaking words in a language Akbar did not understand. He kept touching him the way doctors do. And the girls and boys were all staring at him. He could not summon any courage to look back yet there was a pair of eyes within the crowd, which was not following the trail of the doctor's hand for they were set such immensely on Akbar's face. The eyes of a reader. Reading the stories behind the skins.

The doctor pressed his ribs so hard it gave throbs in his bones. Akbar could feel his skin paling and he could feel the girl reading it. The pain vibrated in the wounds and the slits the hospital had gifted him. And then the doctor released. The ache fading away with every loss of the touch.

He looked at the door. *What if his mother is searching for him? When will this be over? Why does he need to sit naked among so many girls?*

He looked at the girl reading him. Her face turned into a smile. A smile that emits solace. A smile that shows the nature is loving you. A smile as if she understood what

Akbar was feeling. And he didn't doubt that, for he knew the smile was a truth, he knew she understood him even without him saying a word, he knew the magic in reading. And she was reading the silent stories beneath his skin.

It took longer for it to be over. And Akbar was glad to cover his skin again. The doctor was gone. The crowd thinning away. But the girl, like every reader, approached her book.

'You don't like it, do you?' she said in a soft voice.

Akbar stared at her blankly. Just letting her read. For it was easier than speaking.

'I know you don't. Who would?' a sigh, 'Do you read?'

He nodded. 'Only tragedies'

She smiled. 'Then you can find it anywhere embarking any surface of the universe. Why don't you read nature when nature turns against you? Why don't you escape into the hidden meanings of the glyphs around you? Why don't you use the magic a reader has and run away from such realities?'

He looked into her face, beneath her skin. Reading. 'Were you running away too?' he said

She glanced at the walls, 'When I'm in here, I always'

Years later the nights weren't anymore desolate. It weren't ghastly. For when the nights come, Akbar would peer at the sky reading the patterns the stars create and the tales they were hiding.

He didn't know where she was. She didn't know where he was. But they both had parts of each other tethered to them. She gave him words in the night skies. And he gave her a story to immortalize.

BOOK TWELVE: The End Which Begins

LONGISSIMUS DIES CITO CONDITUR

Even the longest day soon
ends

When words end, the stories actually begin.

Your Falling Stars.

All of this is a dream that turns into music into a heartbeat. As real and as inevitable as heartbeats. As the pages end, let the words live.

You may have all heartbeats to listen to. The music on which your blood dances its way in your veins. There is a music in you, readers.

In you.

Of you.

For you.

By you.

The music which is you.

The rhythm of *your* falling stars.

We all have someone. Someone who believes in us. For some they are in the beauties of mothers, for some they are in the shield of fathers, for some they are in the laughter of friends. And for me that someone is in the soldier of my brother.

Can't we have someone?

To have faith in our dreams,

Someone to take risks for our smiles?

Someone to pierce through our faux visages

To reach our heart's realities

Someone to understand,

Someone to sacrifice,

Someone to wipe the tears on our pillow,

Someone to take us

To the place, we want to go.

Someone to festoon our lives

With our ecstasies

Someone to kick away

The abruptness of realities

Someone to not think

What people would say

Someone who in our journeys

Abreast us, along with us, stay?

You could find someone like that

I assure you

Someone who not only love your life

But also hate your cries

Someone who'll take your hand

And make you climb the Everest

No matter the people shout you can fall;

No matter how much the people criticize,

There'll be someone holding your back

Someone to make you rise.

- (Someone)

To all the living souls of this planet,

Death has to arrive.

Struggle to live, o human

Till when will you survive?

In this war to avoid

What inevitably will arrive

In this feeling to fear

The time which inexorably will be near

We forget, o readers

We forget to live the fun.

This marathon which we every day try to run

Our legs will get weary,

We forget death can be avoided by none.

So, what if we die?

Everyone will one day

Why do you think you can run away?

Don't run, o readers, away from death

Run after your chimeras,

Chase the will-o'-the-wisps,

Escape to your own utopia,

Like fire was for Hestia.

Escape not from death

It had reached Earth before

And to you someday it will

O readers,

Au revoir until:

Until comes to us the pain

Until we get united again

- (Au Revoir)

257

Thank you for staying with me through the pages. My readers, it was because of you.

Thank you for helping me through every step. My both brothers, it was because of you.

Thank you for making the stars fall. My Allah, it was because of You.

"The end of the book, the beginning of you."